DATE DUE

Library of
Roger E. Rickson

HEIRS AND REBELS

An early letter from Vaughan Williams to Holst (about 1895).

HEIRS AND REBELS

Letters written to each other
and occasional writings on music

by

RALPH VAUGHAN WILLIAMS

and

GUSTAV HOLST

Edited by
Ursula Vaughan Williams
and
Imogen Holst

NEW YORK
COOPER SQUARE PUBLISHERS, INC.
1974

Originally Published 1959 by Oxford University Press
Reprinted by Permission of Oxford University Press
Published 1974 by Cooper Square Publishers, Inc.
59 Fourth Avenue, New York, New York 10003
International Standard Book Number 0-8154-0487-5
Library of Congress Catalog Card Number 73-86441

Printed in the United States of America

Every man who possesses real vitality can be seen as the resultant of two forces. He is first the child of a particular age, society, convention; of what we may call in one word a tradition. He is secondly, in one degree or another, a rebel against that tradition. And the best traditions make the best rebels.

GILBERT MURRAY

ACKNOWLEDGEMENTS

WE wish to thank Messrs. Macmillan for permission to quote from the article on 'Conducting' in *Grove's Dictionary* (1904) and the Oxford University Press for permission to quote from the preface to *The English Hymnal*: also the British Broadcasting Corporation for allowing us to reprint the article on 'The Composer in Wartime' from *The Listener*; and Yale and Harvard Universities for allowing us to print lectures by Holst.

We are grateful to Miss Joan Pemberton of the Central Music Library, Miss Houlgate of the B.B.C. Reference Library, Miss Barbara Banner of the Royal College of Music Library, Miss Cowles of Morley College, Miss Mary Buxton, Secretary of the Bach Choir, and Dr. Nigel Fortune of the University of London for information they have helped us to obtain.

We are particularly grateful to Miss Clare Mackail for allowing us to reproduce her drawing of Holst, and to the Hon. Mrs. Geoffrey Edwards, Miss Rosamund Strode, and Sir Gilmour Jenkins for the many ways in which they have helped us to prepare the material for this book.

CONTENTS

ILLUSTRATIONS

PREFACE

THE friendship between Ralph Vaughan Williams and Gustav Holst began in 1895 when they first met as students at the Royal College of Music and lasted until Holst's death in 1934. From the very beginning they used to play each other the earliest sketches of whatever music they were writing at the time. Each new work was discussed, pulled to pieces, and even fought over till the issues became clear and the composer was able to find his own way, sometimes in spite of the criticisms, sometimes because of them. This musical bond was so strong that Vaughan Williams used to say that they shared a Muse: they spoke gaily of cribbing from each other and of writing each other's music.

The letters in this volume are fragments of a forty-year-long conversation about music. The two friends met so often that their correspondence, even if it were complete, would seem interrupted and fragmentary. But the collection is far from complete. Holst kept less than fifty letters, Vaughan Williams less than a dozen. They seldom dated them and only three postmarks have survived. It has not always been possible to find dates from internal evidence, and we have been defeated by letters such as this:

Dear Gustav   Thursday
    Thank you v. much.
I have been playing (?) it through & I believe it is going to be beautiful—all except the bar which we have talked about—and which at any rate, is v. much you.

Yrs
R.V.W.

Where we have known which work they were discussing we have been able to date the letter by referring to concert programmes or to Holst's notebooks which he kept from 1912 to 1934. Vaughan Williams's diaries were bare records of engagements and were thrown away at the end of each year. Holst's contained addresses, rough drafts of programmes, timings of works, and headings for lectures, and were therefore kept for reference.

The letters, for all their incompleteness, allow us to see what

ix

it must have felt like to be a young English composer at the beginning of the twentieth century. In 1900 they were still heirs to the Wagnerian tradition, and it was not until some years later that they learned the existence of their own English heritage of folk-song and Elizabethan music. It is difficult for those of us who have been brought up on English music to realize the over-whelming impact its rediscovery had on Vaughan Williams and Holst when they were still in their early thirties.

We have included only those letters which are directly con-cerned with music: the others have already appeared in the biography of Holst* or are to be published in the forthcoming biography of Vaughan Williams. Letters VIII–XI were only discovered after Vaughan Williams's death, too late for inclusion in the re-issue of the Holst biography: they have therefore been reproduced almost in their entirety.

We have sometimes omitted names, remembering that these were private conversations between two people who would never have said anything in public that could hurt the feelings of others.

As in many families or groups of friends, there are traces of a private language and a personal idiom. The frequent use of quotation marks suggests a particular tone of voice; it is possible that some of these were the inflexions of Stanford. The punctua-tion in Vaughan Williams's letters is often non-existent. He always wrote very fast and used many dashes, and allowed the edges of his writing paper to mark the end of a sentence. The missing stops have been added for the sake of clarity.

The occasional writings included in this volume provide a direct link in the interrupted conversations about music. No essay or article has survived from their years at college. It is tantalizing to read in the Royal College of Music records of 1896–7 of the meetings of the Literary and Debating Society, where Vaughan Williams read papers on Purcell and Bayreuth and opened a debate on the motion 'That the Moderate Man is Contemptible', while Holst spoke on 'The Future of English Music' and proposed 'That Academic Training should be Abolished'.

In the early years of the century Vaughan Williams contri-

*Gustav Holst. A biography, by Imogen Holst (Oxford University Press, 1938, re-issued 1958).

buted articles to *The Vocalist* on a wide range of subjects. He
wrote the preface to the *English Hymnal*, having worked for two
years on the book as music editor, and the articles on 'Fugue' and
'Conducting' for the 1904 edition of *Grove's Dictionary*, and
during these years he gave University Extension Lectures on
music, including folk music.

Holst wrote very few articles for publication and only two or
three of his lectures were carefully written out in detail. He
spent so much of his time in teaching that his informal talks on
music were part of his ordinary working day: the frequent
musical illustrations were sung by groups of his pupils or by
members of the audience.

The book ends with a talk to a composers' concourse given by
Vaughan Williams in 1957 which has not been printed before. It
brings the story back to the starting-point: the student who had
been taught by Parry and Stanford looks back after sixty years
and sees with the perspective of time what the first chapter shows
him living through. The heirs had come into their inheritance
and the rebels had led a revolution of greater importance than
they could guess.

February 1959.

U.V.W.
I.H.

RALPH VAUGHAN WILLIAMS

CHRONOLOGY

1872 Born 12 October at Down Ampney, Gloucestershire.
1890 Entered Royal College of Music as a student, September.
1892 Entered Trinity College, Cambridge. Continued weekly lessons at the R.C.M.
1895 Re-entered Royal College of Music. Became organist at St. Barnabas, South Lambeth.
1897 Married Adeline Fisher, 9 October. Went to Berlin and studied with Max Bruch.
1902 Gave University Extension Lectures and wrote articles for *The Vocalist* for several years.
1903 Started to collect folk-songs and wrote the articles on 'Conducting' and 'Fugue' for *Grove's Dictionary* (1904).
1904 Started work on editing *The English Hymnal.*
1908 Studied with Ravel in Paris.
1914 Enlisted in the R.A.M.C. and served as a private in England, France, and Salonika until 1917.
1917 After a period of training in England was commissioned as 2nd Lieut. Royal Garrison Artillery and returned to France.
1918 Became Director of Music, First Army, B.E.F.
1919 Demobilized. Appointed Professor at the Royal College of Music.
1921 Appointed Conductor of the Bach Choir (until 1928).
1922 First visit to America.
1928 Moved from London to Dorking.
1932 Lectured at Bryn Mawr College on National Music.

As this book is concerned with the friendship between the two composers, no dates in Vaughan Williams's life are given after Holst's death in 1934.

GUSTAV HOLST

CHRONOLOGY

1874 Born 21 September at Cheltenham.

1893 Entered the Royal College of Music as a student, May.

1895 Awarded an open scholarship for composition at the R.C.M., February.

1898 Played trombone in the Carl Rosa Opera Company and the Scottish Orchestra (until 1903).

1901 Married Isobel Harrison, 23 June.

1903 Gave up the trombone and began teaching at the James Allen Girls' School (until 1920)

1905 Appointed Musical Director of St. Paul's Girls' School (until 1934).

1907 Appointed Musical Director at the Morley College for Working Men and Women (until 1924).

1918 Appointed Musical Organizer in the Educational Department of the Y.M.C.A. in the Near East (until June 1919).

1919 Appointed Professor at the Royal College of Music (until 1924) and at the University College, Reading (until 1923).

1923 Accident and concussion, February.

1924 Nervous breakdown. A year's rest.

1932 Appointed Lecturer in Composition at Harvard University, for six months. Taken ill in March.

1934 Operation in London on 23 May, after having been an invalid for two years.
Died 25 May.

I

LETTERS 1895-1903

Letter I

> *Vaughan Williams to Holst*
> 19 Second Avenue
> Brighton
> Undated. [Probably 1897]

Dear V.H.

Thanks so much for your letter, your left hand is most admirable—but does it mean that your hand* is still bad—you never said anything about it—this is very wrong of you —I feel pretty stupid today because though it is the sabbath I have been scoring my Mass† all day (it is now 4.30) I am approaching the end of the Credo—

Having now been to sleep for 10 minutes I can continue.

Did I ever tell you of my final talk with Stanford in which we agreed that if I *added* a short movement in E major in the middle & altered the Coda the thing might stand—I had already got an extra movement in E major which I had cut out!

Walküre does sound fine on a Brass band doesn't it. I used to hear a German brass band do it at one of the Earls Court exhibitions. When you come back to London—mind you come to see us *directly* you get back. I am probably going to take my mother to Birdlip next week. I wonder if you will be at Cheltenham by any chance, I think I shall come over and see (if I have an opportunity) whether you are there—also if I can remember where you live. Have you been writing anything or is your hand too bad—why not try looking glass music?

*Holst suffered all his life from neuritis in his right arm.
†An early work, later discarded.

This took me $\frac{1}{4}$ hour!

Have you expedited round Lincolnshire at all—but I expect you just want to sit still between your shows.* I am sorry for you stuck up in that God-forsaken place, can't you get a *band*master's place somewhere? wouldn't that be good—you ought to be able to get one easily after all your experience.

I think H. J. [Wood] must have gone abroad by now—he was going some time soon I know.

Well it will be good when we all meet again in London.

I always thought that working hard in London was bad enough but working hard when you're on a nominal holiday is the devil.

Y————
R.V.W.

I will give you 2d if you can play this on the trombone.

*Holst earned his living during the years 1896–1903 playing the trombone in theatre orchestras (for pantomime), in the White Viennese Band (at seaside resorts) and later in the Carl Rosa Opera Company and the Scottish Orchestra.

Letter II

Vaughan Williams to Holst

Undated. [July 1897]

Dear von Holst

Excuse this paper but I have no other.

I am leaving this damned place in October and going abroad.

Suppose you were offered it* would you consider the matter? The screw is £50 and the minimum duties:

Monday: boys any time after 6.0
Wed: boys 7.0 service 8.0–9.0
Thurs: full practice 8.30 or 8.15 till 10 or past if you
         can get them to stop.
Sunday: 11.0 with choral communion once a month
         7.0 and children's service at 3.0 once a month.

Besides this you are supposed to run the choral society whenever it intermittently exists, and give occasional organ recitals.

Mind I AM NOT OFFERING IT YOU *only* if you would like it I will do my best to Back you.

Will you ANY WAY take my practice and service Wed: Aug 4th at 7.0. Practice Aug. 5 at 8.15 and the services Aug 8th (Sunday) at 11.0 & 7.0 for the usual fee whatever that is?

Then the Vicar could have an opportunity of finding out your merits; he is already rather struck by the way you took that choir practice.

Please answer *at once*

R. Vaughan Williams
2 St. Barnabas Villas
S. Lambeth Rd.
S.W.

*Post of organist at St. Barnabas, South Lambeth.
Directly after their marriage in October 1897 Vaughan Williams and his wife went to Berlin, where *The Ring* was being performed and where he became a pupil of Max Bruch. They remained abroad for several months.

H.R.–B

Letter III

Vaughan Williams to Holst

Undated. [July 1897]

Dear V.H.

The following is an accurate description of your duties next week.

Wed

7.0   Boys

give them a few exercises on [sight?] tests what they're accustomed to then take them through the chants & hymns for Sunday as per list.

8.0   Service

give g. for the Vicar then do not play any Amens but give .C. for 'O Lord open thou our lips' and then accompany as per beastly-blue-book.

Choose one of the Sunday chants for the psalms, the Vicar will tell you which to have. Then play Magnificat (if they do it—ask) to chant 119 and nunc dim to 143 *soft and slow*.

Then give .g. or F♯ for creed and accompany all the responses and the Amens after that ♪♯♩♩ except before the sermon when the Amen for some weird reason is *said*.

Thursday practice the chants & hymns—boys about 8.15 those louts of men will slope in about 8.45 and make you mad—the only ones who can sing will be away; let the boys go by 9.30. If you like you can keep the louts on but there is no necessity.

Sunday, be there by 10.45

1. Short and easy voluntary
2. F♯ —no playing until after Lords prayer when:—
3. C for 'O Lord' etc; do not accompany responses unless there are no tenors or something

the legend itself is concerned) treat the darkness as simply a curious natural phenomenon which had the results which you are about to relate. Secondly you must make the possession of the lamp much more important.

Thirdly you MUST quite remodel the part where it says he couldn't get into the garden with his lamp—making it more *emphatic*—why not say that he met a porter* at the gate who said 'throw away your lamp you will have no use for it in the garden—unless you throw away your lamp you may not enter.'

Now about the style—it is much too loose—do be more careful to say just what you mean and no more. If I were in your place I should read Malory and old ballads and only use words that were used by them. If you use odd words like 'hight' (by the way I can't make sense of that line) you *must* make the rest correspond in style; otherwise it will read like Corder's translation of Wagner. E.g. why say 'all safe' when you might say 'safe' and many other cases. I like your tune extraordinarily (I obeyed you implicitly) except the third line ('a lamp he carried') The first line is I suppose in the Phrygian mode, the 2nd & third certainly modulate and imply harmonies.

(By the way to hark back I don't like 'no ending hath that story' it implies not that the end is torn out but that it goes on for ever.)

I don't quite approve of your martial bit—in itself it is very nice—but surely while the stage issue is vague, you might put in a *lot* of little bits as she looked at the various legends—not only one—and even then it is a kind of miniature painting which is only suitable in a comic opera (e.g. Meistersinger Act I, Eva's remarks about the three Davids or David's recitation of the various 'tones').

I like all the music and voice parts very much. The leading up to the legend is very good—the last two bars are quite beautiful.

I am keeping the music to show to N.G. [Nicholas
*Not a railway porter. [RVW.]

Gatty] when he comes back. H. [Howard] Jones is gone back to Berlin.

There

Y

R.V.W.

N.B. (I mean P.S.) Thanks very much for the shortbread which I hope refers allegorically to your short further absence.

Letter VI

Vaughan Williams to Holst

Undated: no address. [1901?]

My Dear V.

I am ashamed at not having written to you before. I will first thank you for the 'Ave Maria' which I still think beautiful as I always did. I have [been] playing it over and pointing out its beauties to a cousin of mine who sings in the Magpies [Madrigal Society] and have persuaded her to take an interest in it.

I admire 'Sita'* very much—I had some criticisms however to make but I can't remember what they are—and to tell you the truth I feel too lazy tonight to find the drawer where I have put it away.

I think the chief criticism was levelled against the dressing up device—which seems to me rather mechanical and not quite 'rein menschlich' enough. Also it is not quite 'inevitable' enough to fit in with the fatalistic nature of the rest of the plot.

I am alone in my glory at present and likely to be so for some time as my wife is at Brighton looking after her invalid brother and I don't know when she'll be able to leave him.

I have to go to Barnet twice a week now which is an awful nuisance

Y

R.V.W.

*Sita: Holst's three-act opera which he was working on from 1899 to 1906.

PLATE 1

Ralph Vaughan Williams and Gustav Holst (probably 1897)

PLATE 2

Published Compositions by GUSTAV VON HOLST.

SONGS.

The Sergeant's Song (*Words by Thomas Hardy*)
A Song of the Woods
} Willcocks & Co.,
      21a Berners Street, W.

Margarete's Cradle-Song (*Words by H. Ibsen*)
Slumber-Song
} Laudy & Co.,
      139 Oxford Street, W.

Dewy Roses - Chappell & Co., 49 New Bond Street, W.

Invocation to the Dawn - - The Vocalist Company, 27 Fetter Lane, E.C.
    (*Words from the " Rig Veda "*)

PART-SONGS.

Love is enough
Dream Tryst
Thou didst delight my Eyes } - -- Novello & Co., 1 Berners Street, W
Now is the Month of Maying
Ye Little Birds

Light Leaves Whisper (*Madrigal*, 6 *Parts*)
" Ave Maria " (*Female Voices*) } - Laudy & Co., 139 Oxford Street, W.
A Love-Song

Published Compositions by R. VAUGHAN WILLIAMS.

SONGS.

Silent Noon - - - - Willcocks & Co., 21a Berners Street, W.

Orpheus with his Lute
When I am dead, my Dearest } - Keith, Prowse & Co., 48 Cheapside, E.C.

Whither must I wander?
Boy Johnny
Blackmwore by the Stour
If I were a Queen } -- The Vocalist Company, 27 Fetter Lane, E.C.
Tears, Idle Tears
In Linden Lea
The Winter's Willow

PART-SONGS.

Rest (5 *Parts*)
Ring out your Bells (*Madrigal*, 5 *Parts*) } - Laudy & Co., 139 Oxford Street, W.

Sound Sleep (*Female Voices*) - - Novello & Co., 1 Berners Street, W.

Announcement of early published works

Letter VII
Vaughan Williams to Holst
Incomplete: undated: no address. [1901?]
You did tell me about the 'Ave Maria': didn't I refer to it?
I meant to. I've finished my 'Bucolic Suite'* and written a
song and made a rough copy of the score of the Trombone
thing and finished a volume of Purcell† and am starting
another thing called a 'Sentimental Romance'‡
That Glasgow critic is a blasted fool and condemns himself
out of his own mouth.
My dear V. I meant to have said a lot more but I can't
somehow so will compress it all into a comprehensive
'Bless you'.

Yours always
R.V.W.

Letter VIII
Vaughan Williams to Holst
Undated: no address. [1902?]
Dear V.H.
I don't know who the divine Rockfeller is—but I am
going to follow his advice and fill the first part of my letter
with business while the rest shall overflow with sentiment.

Part I Business

The business refers (a) to your songs & (b) to your suite. To
deal first with (a). I must say that the arguments against
publishing at your own expense seem greater than those for
that course—for the following reasons—
(i) If I see a piece of music published by a man *whom I
know nothing else about*, and see those fatal words 'Author's
property' at the bottom of the cover, it at once sets me

---

*Vaughan Williams's *Bucolic Suite*, performed 10 March 1902 at the
Winter Gardens, Bournemouth, by Dan Godfrey.

†*Welcome Odes* edited for the Purcell Society, published 1904–6.

‡Possibly *Symphonic Rhapsody*, performed 7 March 1904 at the
Winter Gardens, Bournemouth, by Dan Godfrey.

against him, makes me think him a poor fellow and pre-
vents me wanting to buy his song—Therefore I am afraid
that if the rest of the world is like me your purchasers will
be limited

(α) To those who know you personally

(β) Those who know you through your music—and
these owing to your extreme youth are at present, though
enthusiastic, yet unfortunately small [in number].

(ii) Novello have just published two part songs of yours and
if these are successful would they not very likely buy some
whole songs from you a little later on—the moral of which
is *wait*.

(iii) I think it most improbable that any pecuniary emolu-
ment would accrue to you from this course—nor, I think,
any fame from songs so to speak privately [This ends a
double sheet: the second sheet is missing.]

Letter IX
Holst to Vaughan Williams
Undated: no address, incomplete: first four pages missing.
[Berlin, 1903]

Holst and his wife had a holiday in Germany
in the summer of 1903; it was his first visit to
a foreign country.

. . . oils. What was the stuff they used before then? In
the evening we went to some friends of Gertrude Pepper-
corn. There was an artist there who told my wife that he
learnt English first from some sailors and some gold diggers
from Australia and was slightly surprised when on his first
speaking English at a dinner party all the ladies promptly
got up and left the room!!! Yesterday (Sunday) I went
ticket buying in the biggest gale (with snow) I ever remember. 'Was ihr wollt' in the afternoon *was* 'Twelfth Night'
and was a failure somehow or other. Rosa Halle spent the
evening with us and we had a good time. Today we had
lunch with Matthias* and his family. Alas! I am learning to

*His second cousin, Matthias von Holst.

swill beer and wine like a native. Afterwards we had an
hour in the National Gallery. Do you know the Arnold
Böcklin room? *Gorgeous.* Nearly all the pictures were
added after your Baedeker came out.

Jesus* sent a post card this morning—I am going to see
Him at 9.30 tomorrow.

Great news—I have written three post cards and two
letters in German! The recipients talk of having them
framed!! Rather a doubtful compliment I fear.

I have been trying to think where we (you and I) are
and where we come in and what we ought to do.

(Being together so much I think we work along in much
the same way but I may be wrong).

To begin with I think we crawl along too slowly—of
course it is something to get along at all and I do think our
progress is very genuine—but there ought to be more.

The 'getting on' theory is damned rot. **** and ****
both spoil themselves by it. It seems to give them a sort of
hardness and I feel so sorry for them both. . . . Don't tell
this to anyone else because it sounds so beastly. Of course
you understand that I am really deeply sorry especially for
****.

I now think the M C C a magnificent idea and I hope it
will grow but as regards our two selves I feel we ought to
do a lot more but cannot think what!

Seeing foreigners is a mistake as a rule. Don't you think
we ought to victimize Elgar? Write to him first and then
bicycle to Worcester and see him *a lot?* I wish we could do
that together. Or else make a list of musicians in London
whom we think worthy of the honour of being bothered by
us and *who have time and inclination to be bothered* and then
bother them. For instance those two fellows that Robin
Legge† raves about. They ought to listen to *all* our stuff

*We have been unable to identify the German musician who was
known by this nickname.
†Robin Legge, 1862–1933. At this time assistant music critic of *The
Times.*

and we to all theirs. It would be dreadful while it lasted but
I think the effect would be good.

Somehow we seem too comfortable—we don't seem to
strain every nerve. Anyhow I know I don't. And composing
is a fairly impossible affair as things go even at the best of
times. While I think of it, is Henry J [Wood] open to
victimizing? We ought never to send anything to him by
post if it can be avoided but always to see him.

I don't know whether you are in the same box but I feel
I want to know a lot of poets and painters and other fearful
wild fowl.

As for opera I am bewildered. 'Die Feuersnot' is in reality
quite simple and unoriginal *as opera*. Charpentier's
'Louise' is idiotic as opera. And I do feel sometimes inclined
to chuck Sita in case it is only bad Richard I [Wagner].
Unless one ought to follow the latter until he leads you to
fresh things. What I feel is that there is *nothing* else but
Wagner excepting Italian one act horrors.

As for conducting (which we ought to learn) it is impossible to attain in England and I fear we must give up all
hopes of it. As an orchestral player I really do feel sorry, as
England is crying out (unconsciously) for real conductors.
Henry J. is the nearest approach . . . *And it is not all a
question of unlimited rehearsals.*

Your last letter was the result of thinking matters over—
this is a poor return as it is the result of waking up too early
in the morning and trying to go to sleep unsuccessfully! So
you must excuse if I write more than my usual allowance
of rot.

Of course the matter is made rather worse for me owing
to lack of cash and I feel more and more that my mode of
living is very unsatisfactory. It is not so bad in London say
during the 'French Milliner' when I did a fair amount of
writing every day but the Worm* is a wicked and loath-
some waste of time. Yet the only alternative I know of is
stick wagging for one of George Edwardes' touring com-

*Stanislas Wurm was the conductor of the White Viennese Band.

panies. People who are victims of the 'getting on' theory always advise this but if one does it at all one must do it properly and then good bye to music!

There is also the theory that one should get rich first and then compose.

When I was a child my father told me that Sterndale Bennett worked out that theory during his life very satisfactorily. When I was older I heard Sterndale Bennett's music. . . .

Getting rich requires a 'teshneek' of its own that some people learn slowly and others never. I don't know which class I belong to and don't care. There is no time to learn that *and* composition. Not that I believe one should cram theory from childhood. But that once having started (after school etc is over) an Englishman may think himself lucky if, after hard work, he writes anything decent before he is fifty. For now I have been abroad I see what a terrible lot we have to contend against in England.

And I also feel that there is no time for pot-boiling. As tromboning is so damnably uncertain I must do it but it is really bad for one I am sure. I almost feel I can now trace its evil effect in Tchaikowsky but it is a very insiduous disease.

Still I think it would be a great thing for me if I could always live in London and say goodbye to the Worm (by the bye I must try and get a summer engagement from him for my return in July or August!) and all seaside bands. I should be sorry to leave the Scottish for some things but it really would be better on the whole. But this is all off the main point.

If money matters were quite satisfactory with me I still should be just as puzzled as to what you and I ought to do— money matters only make things worse.

I think we are 'all right' in a mild sort of way. But then mildness is the very devil. So something must happen and we must make it happen.

While I remember—the voice parts of your opera are

impossible. You must not do this sort of thing. Don't show them to a singer but *get singers to sing them*. Then recollect that singing in an opera house means twice as much exertion. I think you will be convinced.

I hope our letters will not cross any more—send me one *soon*. Our time is up next Monday but my wife wants to stop on while this jolly blizzard lasts as we are more or less at home in Berlin. I will let you know when we have decided and everything will be forwarded from here.

Yours Ever

G v H

Letter X

Holst to Vaughan Williams

Berlin. [1903]

Dear R V W   Monday

I went to Jesus* but I didn't drink. He was awfully nice and kept me an hour and a half. But he said that the tune at the end of the Drapa† and the 'Invocation'‡ were written too much in the 'popular English style' to be of any use in Germany. In fact he seemed to think that I had written both things in order to suit Messrs Chappel & Co. If I had time I would tell you about an awful German-American professor that he took me to but that must wait as I have so much to say that is more important, for the professor turned out to be an utter fraud.

Now then to business.

I really cannot feel concerned about your fears that all your invention has gone. I am sorry but it is impossible. You got into the same state of mind just before you wrote the Heroic Elegy so that I look on it as a good sign and quite expect to hear that you have struck oil when you write again.

---

*See footnote on page 11.

†*Ornulf's Drapa*. Scena for baritone and orchestra, written 1898.

‡*Invocation to Dawn*, the earliest of his settings of hymns from the Rig Veda, for which he made his own translations from the Sanskrit, 1902.

I have thought about it a good deal and these are some of my conclusions.

1) You have never lost your invention but it has not developed enough. Your best—your most original and beautiful style or 'atmosphere' is an indescribable sort of feeling as if one was listening to very lovely lyrical poetry. I may be wrong but I think this (what I call to myself the *real* R V W) is more original than you think.

But when you are not in this strain, you either write 'second class goods' or you have a devil of a bother to write anything at all. The latter state of mind may seem bad while it lasts but it is what you want to make yourself do for however much I like your best style it must be broadened. And probably it is so each time you get into a hopeless mess. Probably you are right about mental concentration—that is what you want more than technique. For that reason perhaps lessons would do you good but it would be a surer way to try and cultivate it 'on your own'.

In one of Parry's lectures he played all the sketches Beethoven made for the 'Eroica' Funeral March (first theme). Sketch no 1 was not at all bad. No 3 was beautiful. No 6 was stupid. No 9 was bloody. *The final one was a return to no 3.* The moral of which is that if you spoil good stuff by working at it you must spoil the spoilation by more work. Of course waiting plays a small part but I think you are wrong in thinking that working at a theme or idea will ruin it. Even suppose the working out is not so good as the original you can always go back and then you will have the result of your experience into the bargain.

I know there is a good deal to be said for the other side but I think that the only true waiting for ideas is the waiting or resting after a long spell of hard work.

Then again when you spoil good ideas is not that because you write too much—that is you go ahead too fast—instead of grinding away bar by bar which is the only true hard work?

Would it be good, do you think, for you to rewrite as a matter of course *everything* you write about six months after it is finished? (*Really* finished, not merely sketched). Whenever I have re-copied or re-scored anything, I have improved it very much. Anyhow I would never score at once—wait until your mud pie is hardened and until you can compare it in cold blood to others.

Another idea of mine is madder and perhaps even harmful but anyhow you shall have it. Cannot invention be developed like other things? And would not it be developed by your trying to write so many themes every day? Three decent themes a day for instance (probably in trying, you would get a few more that were verging on indecency). Then at the end of a week you could see how many were worth anything.

I am sure I am right about us being too comfortable. When you work hard you merely cover a lot of ground instead of making sure of your ground as you go on. (This is not *absolutely* true but I think you have a tendency that way).

Another thing we must guard against and that is getting old! Especially you—I am more juvenile than ever, I think, but I have my doubts about you. As I said before we have so much to contend against and in England there is no one to help, so that progress is sure to be a bit erratic. For instance, I doubt whether your Rhapsody will sound half as good as the Elegy and if you feel old you will be disappointed. Whereas the real truth is the Elegy was a climax and the Rhapsody a new start—a broadening-out—which will in the long run probably do you far more good.

As for me I think I have got careless owing to Worming and pot-boiling. For I am certain that Worming is very bad for one—it makes me so sick of everything so that I cannot settle down to work properly. And pot-boiling *as I have done it* is bad because I got into the way of thinking that anything would do. Whereas we must write now chiefly so that we may write better in the future. So that every detail of everything we do must be as perfect as possible. For the next few years not only ought we to write more carefully than we have ever done before but more carefully than we need ever write again. My wife has had another idea which I think I shall adopt. That is that when we return I shall not take any Worming job or go out of London until the Scottish begins. If I can get a theatre well and good, if not I will even accept your offer of lending me money rather than play two or three times a day. (You see our living in London is pretty cheap). Then I should like to try to work systematically from August to November both at writing and studying music. I rather think you know more music than I do, anyhow I am sure I don't know enough about Beethoven's sonatas or Schubert's songs and heaps of other things. I wonder if it would be possible to lock oneself up for so many hours every day. If so it would be far easier for me than for you as you have so many friends. I feel it would be so splendid to 'go into training' as it were, in order to make one's music as beautiful as possible. And I am sure that after a few months' steady grind we should have made the beginning of our own 'atmospheres' and so should not feel the need of going abroad so much. For it is all that makes up an 'atmosphere' that we lack in England. I am sorry I have to make such a commonplace remark. Here people actually seem anxious to hear new music, still more wonderful, they even seem anxious to find out all about a new composer! That in itself would work a revolution in England.

By the bye I am certainly going to rewrite the words of Sita as you suggest. They are disgraceful and that was largely due to Worming etc. I used to write them at odd moments, often in the orchestra.

Which reminds me—one may get hold of a decent theme on the top of a bus etc but I deny utterly that one can do 'splendid work' there—especially the work we most need. I used to be proud of writing things at odd times. It was great fun but it was damned rot and it helped on my present

carelessness. I should like to keep up this sort of correspondence all the time I am away. Don't you think it might
do us good? Only you must tell me more about yourself.

One problem puzzles me. Is it really bad to write at the
piano? I try one or the other as it suits me best. If it is bad,
wherein does the badness lie and what bad results accrue
from it?

Do you think it would be good to give ourselves a small
dose of what Wagner had—analysing a sonata and then
writing one in the same style and form? Anyhow don't you
start counterpoint—it's the thing after that that we need.
Also you might follow the advice you gave me—to cultivate
a more leisurely frame of mind when composing. Perhaps
you don't need it so much as I do but I think you do in
another way. Namely you must feel young (you are
absurdly young for a composer and for an *English* composer you are hardly hatched!) and if a thing does not come
off after a day's or a week's working, then that working
will make its due effect when you are grown up.

I wish you could have a holiday now, and then have a
grind like I propose doing—that is, if you think it a good
plan. It would be more fun if we both did it together
although perhaps there is nothing in it.

After much deliberation we have decided not to bicycle to
Dresden and probably not from there to Munich. What do
you think about the latter? I think we can neither spare the
money or the time. The latter is especially important as we
must see the Tyrol. Also a long ride like that would mean
getting into training beforehand and a lot more rest afterwards for which we have no time as I think it more important to see operas, pictures, people, and cities than the
country barring the Tyrol. Of course we shall have short
rides. Address till I write again

Poste Restante, Dresden.

Yours Ever

G v H

Letter XI

Holst to Vaughan Williams

[1903. Dresden?]

Tuesday

Dear R V W

I really don't know what to say about the rhapsody parts excepting that I have walked my wife off her legs day after day until she was too tired to do any copying. While lately I am sorry to say she has not been very well. Also she does not seem able to acquire a 'teshneek' but can only do it very slowly so that these few pages we send you really represent rather a lot of work. I have only been able to correct the two first flutes. On p. 6, last bar but one, surely you mean C for Fl I and not E. But if so why have you scratched out C? I have *not* corrected that but in other places I have filled in a few accidentals.

Please don't be very disgusted with us. I must drop this now as I have such a heap to write about.

I hope you bear in mind that all the rot I write is merely a collection of stray thoughts. Well to begin with what the Hell do you mean by talking about premature decay and getting fat?

I meant 'getting old' in the sense of 'becoming mature' —that is when progress either stops or becomes slower. We must not get old for the next forty years because we have such a stiff job and (1) you sometimes have said that you feel that 'it is time you did something' after all these years —I forget your exact words but I have felt the same myself often but it is *rot*. We are not old enough and we have not had enough training *of the right sort* (I am coming to that.)

(2) Sometimes when anything turns out an awful failure it may teach us more than a thundering success—it does not follow that it *will* but it *may*—which would be of little use if one was growing old.

So for these two reasons and for the further one that we have so much to learn and it is so difficult to find out how

H.R.–C

to learn it, we must regard ourselves as very 'E♭' chickens *

As I told you once before, Richard II [Strauss] seems to me to be the most 'Beethovenish' composer since Beethoven. Perhaps I am wrong but anyhow you will agree that whatever his faults, he is a real life composer.

As far as I can make out his training seems to have been

(1)
Bach, Mozart, Beethoven
(2)
Schumann and Brahms
(3)
Wagner.

Mine has been:
(1)
Mendelssohn
(2)
Grieg
(3)
Wagner

This alone speaks volumes.

Richard II had such a terrific classical training that Brahms and Wagner never lifted him off his feet.

Whereas I (as you say of yourself) 'don't seem to fit on to their music at all'. (Mozart and Beethoven). And I believe, as you once said about Richard II himself, that one ought to be able to feel that every composer is the result of those that have gone before him. So we must begin by feeling it about ourselves.

Now if you can prove to me that all this is nonsense I shall be only too delighted as it is a serious thing to discover and if true it means years and years of *extra* study with the usual lot thrown in.

If it is true there is no one in England to teach us as far as I know. Twelve years ago Parry would have been the man.

*E♭=small (from the size of E♭ clarinet and cornet).

PLATE 3

Ralph Vaughan Williams with Parry

PLATE 4

Holst at work, as his pupil Clare Mackail imagined him

As far as I can tell, McCunn* has a lot to learn from you.

If you really must have lessons in London I sometimes think that Stanford is the only man now that he has learnt the elements of good manners towards you. *But I don't want you to go to him.*

Could not you go to H.J.W. once every two months or so and get his opinion on all you have written? (Paying him of course.)

But I believe that really the only good that will last will be done by struggling away on your own. Stanford is all crotchets and fads and moods although the latter have improved. And that healthy vigorous beefsteak optimism of Parry is a delusion that blinds one to the real difficulties in the way. When under a master I instinctively try to please him whereas our business is to learn to please ourselves which is far more difficult as it is so hard to find out what we want.

I thought that perhaps trying to write so many themes every day might possibly develop one's invention but I expect that is all nonsense. Anyhow I can think of no other way.

I have been trying to make up my mind as to what is the best way of settling down to compose. On the whole I think the chief ingredients are:

(1) Hard work. (But not this *alone* as I have always thought until now—as you say, one cannot be always composing.)

(2) Having just the very best art of all kinds.

(3) Complete change from music. To be divided into (a) other work or exercise, and (this is most important) (b) *Absolute laziness.*

All this sounds cheap and obvious but unless you can assure me that it is false there are one or two conclusions to be drawn from it. To begin with, 'Worming' is absolutely criminal. One gets wearied out by false art—becomes

*Hamish McCunn, Scottish composer (1868–1916).

saturated by it in fact. It is bad enough when I get sick of it but it is worse when I enter into the spirit of it and enjoy it in a beastly sort of way. May be one ought to do something besides composition, but it ought to be something *outside* music I think.

Then you once said you were so ashamed of yourself because your life seemed all holiday. Now if you find that you write better for going away into the country now and then, then it is your D U T Y to go and do so. Again, are you able to discover what helps you in composition and what takes your thoughts entirely away from music? For instance, I think walking *always* sets me thinking of new tunes etc whereas bicycling drives all music away. Both are necessary, because when one is not actually writing or mentally composing one should not mentally *drivel* on about music as I do so often. When I thought that composition was merely hard work I used to worry about it in an irritating sort of way and I believe you do the same sometimes. Whereas if I am right we must drop music altogether every now and then so that we never feel stale when we write.

I am more determined than ever to 'go into training' only I want to make sure first what that will consist of.

Systematic planning out of the day or anything approaching it is surely out of the question. We must be more thorough when we play each other our things and we ought to play each one two or three times over at each meeting until the other one knows it thoroughly. The only drawback is that whenever we are together I have always such a lot to talk about!

I have just remembered another point as regards not getting old. It is quite possible that while cultivating concentration of mind you may spoil one or two ideas—anyhow you say you have done so. But that is quite worth it if you don't want any immediate results. It is like stropping the razor before shaving.

The music has gone today (Wednesday) by special permission of the German authorities. It cost 1.45. If it is the same to you we would rather not have the money until we return. There is a slip to be pasted on to the 2nd flute.

Are you quite sure that analysing a Beethoven sonata and then writing one in the same form would not be good? Wagner did it (see 'Grove') and he was the greatest master of form and also one of the most original of all composers. Besides is it not what all painters and poets do? It seems much more sensible to me than more counterpoint.

As for pictures I am quite bewildered. I cannot see the great beauty of Veronese. On the whole I think I like Correggio better than him. But somehow or other my chief delights are the very old pictures—Van Eyck, Holbein, Weyden, Conegliano, Botticelli and Mantegna etc. I seem to 'feel' them so much more easily than I do Rubens or Veronese. I put it down to the fact that I am only beginning to enjoy pictures and I hope to grow to the others in time— perhaps you can help me. Of course the Sistine Madonna is a thing by itself. I nearly went through the roof when I first caught sight of it. But it bothers me to think that I prefer Van Eyck to Rubens etc.—I feel like the curate who only likes the Messiah and the Elijah still I suppose it is all right as long as I don't stop as I am. Everything must have a beginning. We go to Munich on Friday.

Yours
G v H

Letter XII

Holst to Vaughan Williams

Munich [1903]
Saturday

Dear R V W

We remain here until next Saturday when we bicycle into the Tyrol for a week only and then come home to England. Do you think that is sensible? It will leave me

enough money to do without a Worms job so that I can
stick at home and write. Munich is *lovely* and so very un-
English. We thought of biking to one of the lakes but not
too far away though. Do you know any of them? If so just
send me a post card with any bit of advice you can give. We
should like boating and bathing above everything else.

Sunday

This is going to be a 'continued in our next' letter. I sent
a Wedding March to Howard [Jones] which I hope he got in
time. Last night we went to Brand!!! We crawled home
feebly after it in a state of collapse. It was done in the
Schauspielhaus—do you know it? It is a new theatre and by
far the most beautiful one I have ever seen. We go to Faust
on Monday at the new Wagner theatre. Also there is an
opera company from Milan coming on Tuesday. I want to
see Puccini's 'Manon Lescaut' and Donizetti's 'Lucia' done
by real live Italians in their own way. Then on Friday we
finish up with 'Rosmersholm' at the Schauspielhaus. At the
opera we have seen Otello and a first-rate Meistersinger.
As regards the parts, if you don't do the Rhapsody at
College may my wife finish the copying on our return?
Now then!

I quite agree about having things done—the more the
merrier excepting when C V S ruins things at orchestra.*
Do that cantata by all means. Strange to say I decided to try
and write one when we were in Berlin only I don't know of
any words. I am sure the feeling of the coming actual performance will be good for us. As regards the classics, I was
not thinking so much about details of technique as of the
'other thing'. I think that if we were throughly grounded
in the classics we should not be carried away so much by
every new German composer. But I suppose that that is
nonsense because Sterndale Bennet, Parry and Stanford
probably knew as much about the classics as Wagner or

*Stanford took the orchestral class at the R.C.M. while they were
students. Later, both Holst and Vaughan Williams had several of their
early works performed at Patron's Fund Concerts there.

Strauss. Anyhow I feel sure that I don't know nearly as much Beethoven as you do, especially as regards the chamber music.

Now as regards details of technique I fear I have never given them sufficient thought. And as it is always good to know one's weak points this is where you are again ahead of me. In fact this question of climaxes rather bewilders me and I shall have to leave it alone until I return. As to *how* to study I feel rather floored again. But what I personally should like would be to have all Beethoven's chamber music at my fingers' ends as Wagner apparently had: to be able to wallow in it—to soak it in and make it part of one's being. That is my idea. I wish we were better players for then the Cowley Str Wobblers* would be of great use.

I know that awful kind of laziness you speak of. It is the very devil. But when it is very strong I almost think that it is best to give way to it. One little dodge I sometimes try in order to cure it is to play a lot of my old stuff for ten minutes or so, so as to settle my mind on composition.

As to writing at boiling point. This is the only thing I feel fairly certain about. Writing at boiling point is T H E very worst way of composing. Whenever I have done it, it has *always* turned out badly and the only good that ever came of it was when I was able to work the stuff up afresh the next day into something fairly presentable. It *may* be different with you but anyway I wouldn't worry about it.

Before I left Dresden I really managed to see the beauty of Veronese and I think a Rubens crowd is terrific. I always understood that Titian and Raphael were a kind of painters' Bach and Beethoven. But barring the Sistine I cannot see it all. I like Francia etc much better. By the bye is it my fault or is it a fact that in all creation there is nothing so absolutely

*An amateur string quartet which met in a house in the street where Vaughan Williams lived: Nicholas Gatty played violin, Vaughan Williams viola, and his wife cello: we do not know who was the fourth player.

and appallingly BLOODY as the average modern German picture. The New Pinakothek is an exaggerated nightmare to me.

Yours

G v H

II

VAUGHAN WILLIAMS'S EARLY
WRITINGS ON MUSIC

GOOD TASTE

(Reprinted from *The Vocalist* of May 1902)

GOOD taste is, without doubt, the stumbling block in the path of the 'Young English school of composers.' These 'rising young musicians' lack neither good teachers nor good models, nor good concerts, nor good opportunities of bringing their works to a hearing; nevertheless, all their promise seems to be nipped in the bud by the blighting influence of 'good taste.'

What is good taste? Is it a quality ever ascribed to a really great artist? Do we ever say of Beethoven or Mozart that their music is in good taste? And why is this? Because good taste is a purely artificial restriction which a composer imposes on himself when he imagines—rightly or wrongly —that his inspiration is not enough to guide him. A genius has no time to consider the claims of good taste; he is hurried blindly forward by the power of his own invention, and it is only when that fails he feels the absence of that prop on which the weak-kneed habitually stay themselves. What 'minor poet' among musicians would make such a fool of himself as to write the 'Battle of Vittoria'? What well-brought-up composer but would blush for shame to have thought of anything so vulgar as some of Schubert's tunes? Yet how much would they not give to have invented one bar of 'Erlkönig' or the A Major Symphony?

The truth is that the young Englishman is too musicianly. The 'musicianly' composer has studied the whole anatomy of inspiration, and has found out all the mechanical means by which beautiful music is produced. Equipped with this knowledge, he proceeds to build up compositions with yard-measure and plumb-line, quite forgetting that no man can make a living body out of dead clay unless he has first stolen some of the heavenly fire. Many a young composer has stifled his natural impulses in the desire to be musicianly. If he has elected to be 'romantic' he considers himself lost unless he crushes all his power of invention under an entanglement of trombones and bass tubas—and all because Wagner's special inspiration required special expression. If he favours the 'classical' school, he thinks it only becoming to make a show of exercising Brahms's self-restraint, without considering what a storehouse of invention Brahms possessed out of which to deny himself.

It has been said that education is what a man has learnt and forgotten. The musicianly musician is only half educated; he has learnt, but he has not forgotten.

'He that is froward let him be froward still.'

If a composer is naturally vulgar, let him be frank and write vulgar music instead of hedging himself about with an artificial barrier of good taste. If he is naturally trivial, let him not simulate a mock solemnity which is quite foreign to his nature. If every composer will be himself, his music will at all events be genuine. If it is of bad grain, no amount of veneer can alter its nature; if it is good oak it will not be improved by being made to look like mahogany.

Away, then, with good taste. Good taste is the heritage of critics, and a good critic is, proverbially, a bad composer. What we want in England is *real* music, even if it be only a music-hall song. Provided it possess real feeling and real life, it will be worth all the off-scourings of the classics in the world.

BACH AND SCHUMANN

(Reprinted from *The Vocalist* of June 1902)

'Bach and Jean Paul Richter,'* what a contrast! Jean Paul the humorous sentimentalist, and Bach 'the man who wrote fugues,' considered a pedant by the ignorant, and ignorant, by the pedants; and yet the writer, who first connected these two names in one sentence, did so, not for the purpose of violent contrast, but with a clear feeling of their affinity—'Bach and Jean Paul,' writes Schumann, 'had the greatest influence on me.'

There are at the present time very few musicians who think that Bach is merely learned, or that learning and emotion cannot go hand in hand. Nevertheless, even now the whole nature of Bach's work is often misunderstood, and even a well-known writer can write of the 'old fashioned sweetness' of the *Wohltemperierte Klavier*, and considers that 'the spirit of Bach is far enough removed from romance.' But it cannot be mere coincidence that Bach's music, which had so long lain dormant, underwent such a revival in the time of Schumann; nor can the famous performance of the St. Matthew Passion Music under Mendelssohn be dismissed as the unearthing of a fine but forgotten work. It was, in truth, at once the symbol and the proof of the close bond of unity which existed between the Leipzig schools of the seventeenth and nineteenth centuries—a unity not of form only, but of spirit also; so that when Schumann acknowledged his indebtedness to Bach he was not simply naming his counterpoint master, but was indicating the true founder of the romantic school.

It would be a poor argument to claim Bach as the inventor of musical romanticism, merely on the ground that Schumann admired him; even the fact that Schumann was confessedly influenced by him is at best a circuitous course to adopt; but there is no need to use these unconvincing

*Jean Paul Richter (1763–1825). Usually known by his pen name Jean-Paul. A German writer of romantic, humorous, and picaresque works.

proofs when we have the master's own works to show us of
what quality he is. If Bach has anything to do with the
writers of musical romance, we can discover the resemblance
by examining his compositions and judging if the same
forces had weight with him which afterwards influenced
the composers whom we call 'romantic.' ·

The surest means of finding out the nature of a writer's
bent is to notice what medium of expression comes most
naturally to him. What then, was Bach's favourite means
of expression? And is this medium a romantic one or not?
To the first of these questions the answer is not doubtful.
Bach's name is indissolubly connected with the fugue, not
the fugue of the pedant with its triple counterpoint and its
'Stretto Maestrale,' but the fugue in its living and artistic
aspect, expanded so as to include all musical forms in which
the different phases of one idea are brought one after
another under review amidst conditions of ever-increasing
excitement.

Surprising as it may seem, it is nevertheless the fact that
the fugue as exemplified by Bach is a most perfect romantic
medium. The essential difference between a fugue and a
movement in 'sonata form,' is that the fugue consists of the
repetition of one musical phrase on different planes, and in
different surroundings, while the sonata movement consists of several musical subjects which are set off against one
another so as to form a decorative pattern. In the fugue
there is one idea, in the sonata-movement several, and
from this it follows that in a fugue there is one *mood*, and
in a sonata-movement several.

Now this is just the difference which exists between the
classical and romantic in music. In literature the classical
writers may be said, broadly speaking, to give more atten-
tion to beauty of style, while the romantic devote themselves to beauty of subject and sentiment; the subject or
mood of any piece must be homogeneous, but the style pure
and simple depends for its effect on contrast and variety.
Now in 'absolute' music there is no distinction between

subject and style; indeed, abstract music may be said to be all style; in this art only is it possible to obtain that simple delight in beauty for its own sake which makes an united whole out of a decorative scheme of contrast and repetition; thus the sonata form is the most natural means of purely musical expression, but immediately any extraneous 'thought' or 'subject' is added to absolute music it becomes necessary to consider unity of mood; this is the problem which faced Schumann and the other writers of romantic music. For them the purely musical scheme in which equal importance is given to several themes in coordination was unsuitable; the form which was suitable was that in which one idea dominates a whole work—in fact, the fugue. In the most romantic of all his compositions, the Fantasia in C, Schumann preserves the unity of mood by means of a poetical idea which occurs again and again in varied surroundings. To what other origin can this scheme be traced than the Bach fugue, and what better superscription could be written over a Bach fugue than Schumann's very motto:—

> 'Durch alle Töne tönet
> In bunten Erdentraum
> Ein leiser Ton gezogen
> Für den, der heimlich lauschet?'

Bach and Schumann stand on common ground in the way in which they regarded musical form; musical form is essentially decorative, and a composer who looks on the decorative side of music merely as a means will not be likely to add much to the development of music from the constructive point of view. Bach was no inventor in the matter of form; he did not, like Schumann, experience any difficulty in manipulating any form which he chose to employ, but he was content to use the forms ready to hand, such as the Aria, from which he did not even eliminate the Da Capo. Not that Bach was no innovator, but his very innovations show the romantic bent of his mind. His amazing harmonic progressions, which sound new and strange even now, are not the result of any conscious constructive aim, but are the direct outcome of the emotional intensity of the moment. This highly coloured polyphony is what Schumann inherited from Bach, as the most direct and personal expression of the moods inspired by Jean Paul, and this personal factor in their music unites under one banner the composers of 'Widmung' and 'Erbarme dich.' There can be no doubt as to this personal element; music can be absolutely sublime and universal, or absolutely human and personal. Both ways of regarding the art have produced glorious results, but the glory of the one can never be the glory of the other.

One small but not unimportant romantic factor, which appears both in Bach and Schumann, is musical symbolism. We have only to compare the 'Lettres Dansants' of the Carnaval with the 'Lass ihn kreuzigen' of the St. Matthew Passion to be aware that the same impulse acted on each composer. This symbolism is not a mere mechanical device, nor is it claimed for Bach and Schumann that they invented it. Many composers before Schumann had made musical phrases out of their friends' names. Bach only adopted a device made common by his predecessors, but in the hands of a master it ceases to be a mere trick and represents a real emotion. Bach expresses the poignancy of 'Let him be crucified,' in the cross-shaped subject which he uses; and Schumann, in his musical acrostics, has a much deeper purpose than a mere coincidence of letters and notes.

There are of course other composers than Schumann who are called 'romantic.' These, it is true, have little in common with Bach. Schubert and Weber were influenced by Beethoven and the Italians, if by anyone; and no one has ever accused Berlioz of being under the spell of a fugue writer. Indeed, Bach had little to do with the material, and often superficial, romanticism of storms and wild huntsmen and processions to the scaffold. But there is a truer and deeper romance than that of the heart, which deals, not with external events, but with the minds and souls of human beings. This is the romance which Bach shares with his great apostle, Schumann—the romance which, by making the ideal art subservient to the intimacies of the human emotions, finally raises human emotions to the level of ideal art. If it is true that Beethoven and Brahms have caught the 'divine Cecilia's' mantle, and can 'draw an angel down' from heaven, no less is it true that Bach and Schumann have inherited the gift of old Timotheus and 'raise a mortal to the skies.'

LIBRETTOS

(Extracts from 'The Words of Wagner's Music Dramas', *The Vocalist*, June 1902)

A musical drama must, of course, deal with such subjects as come within the scope of music. Now, the nature of music is that it can express emotion, but cannot touch reason and fact. Words, on the other hand, cannot express emotion, but can only indicate emotion through the medium of fact. . . . Drama must have words as well as music, since it must, to a certain degree, appeal to the understanding; the words will, so to speak, locate and crystallize the emotions of the music; but these words, it is to be remembered, must be sung, not spoken. Their business is to express a fact, but this fact must as often as possible be capable of an emotional interpretation, in order that it may be expressed in music. In short, the ideas in a musical drama must be such as a man can feel, and not such as he can only intellectually perceive. To make this possible, the plot of a musical drama must be very little dependent on facts. The action must be founded on the axioms of life, and not on the accidents of circumstances; for, as soon as reason and fact become part of the scheme, then song must abdicate in favour of speech. . . . Where the music needs no help it would be most presumptuous of the words to offer their well-meant but clumsy assistance. There are innumerable cases where music can explain the drama with no extraneous assistance. . . .

What remains for the words to achieve? The duty of the words is to say just as much as the music has left unsaid and no more. Now music, expressing, as we have seen, emotion only, will demand least of the words at the most emotional moments, and the words will stand out most clearly in those explanatory passages where the music is all but non-existent. Therefore the relative importance of words and music will vary exactly as the dramatic situation approximates to feeling or mere explanation. At one end of the scale are those passages where the words are a bare statement of fact; in which case the singer's utterances will be a near approach to speaking, and the orchestra will be almost silent. At the other end are those passages where the music rises to the height of lyrical intensity, and the words merely supplement the music by giving utterance to the human voice. . . . The one thing that is not wanted for a musical drama is 'musical verse.' A decorative scheme of artificial metres and rhymes makes the most unsuitable word-book imaginable. That librettists of all times and countries have hailed from Grub Street, is a truism of musical history: but, contemptible as nearly all librettos are, their real defect lies in their utter unsuitability for musical treatment, both in subject and in style. The reason of this failure is that librettists, good and bad, have always regarded the opera from the standpoint of the spoken play; when they found that a good play was unsuitable they merely substituted a bad one! The fundamental nature of the mistake has been seen more clearly in modern times, when occasionally an accomplished and painstaking librettist has turned out an opera book in faultless Shakespearian style, consisting of a series of neat decasyllables and well-groomed lyrics which would be ludicrous if they were not so pathetic.

Who, then, is to write the words of a musical drama? The task is not an easy one. The words of the drama, important though they be, are yet quite subordinate. They must not appear important by themselves, but only when united to the music. Who shall write poetry which shall fulfil these conditions? A poet who would undertake such work must be at a low ebb of invention. If he is to write poetry worthy of the name, he must not subordinate it to any outside conditions. He cannot entirely sink himself to serve the genius of another; or if he does so, he will be obliged to stick to such commonplaces as are sure not to be unsuitable, and from such commonplaces no good music can spring, unless, indeed, the composer, like Beethoven in *Fidelio*, practically disregards the words, and writes music to a parallel tragedy of a much deeper nature.

There is only one man who can write the words of a musical drama, and that man is the composer of the music, for the drama must generate in the music. If the music is beautiful and noble, then no more need be demanded of the words than that they should help the music, provided always that words and music spring from the same mind and the same inspiration.

Note:

These extracts are the general principles; the rest of the article gives examples and illustrations of their application. When he came to write operas himself, Vaughan Williams modified some of his opinions. With Harold Child (*Hugh the Drover*) and Evelyn Sharp (*The Poisoned Kiss*) he helped with the structure of the story, and he altered details when the writers suggested words or lines or verse-forms that he found uncomfortable for music. Synge's *Riders to the Sea* he took as it stood, cutting a few sentences only. The book for *Sir John in Love* he made for himself from *The Merry Wives of Windsor* (one of the plays for which he had arranged and conducted the music for Benson at Stratford), adding many lyrics from other Elizabethan poets to the text. *Pilgrim's Progress* was mostly Bunyan, but psalms and other biblical passages were used where he wanted something more sustained, e.g. Watchful's song, and the

bird's song; additional material was also used in Vanity Fair.
He never changed his opinion on the point that words must
serve the music, and that they are only of great importance when
they carry the action forward or tell the audience a fact.

CONDUCTING

(The following passage from the article on 'Conducting' by
Vaughan Williams comes from the 1904 edition of *Grove's
Dictionary of Music and Musicians*, and has not been reprinted
in the edition of 1954. It relates to letters in Chapter I.)

The latest important event in the history of English
conducting has been the formation in 1897 of The Queen's
Hall Orchestra under the conductorship of Mr. Henry J.
Wood. This orchestra is not yet (1904) permanent in the
best sense—that is, its members are not exclusively en-
gaged—nevertheless, it is a step in the right direction. The
great reputation of the orchestra, apart from the individual
excellence of its members, is due to the training it has
received from its conductor; and while he has taught his
orchestra Mr. Wood has taught himself, and may now be
reckoned as a first-rate conductor, not of one style alone, but
of all. He has conclusively proved that an Englishman can
become a good conductor if he has the proper opportunities,
and striking as Mr. Wood's abilities are, one cannot help
believing that there are many young English musicians
who would become very capable conductors if they only had
the means of learning the art. Conducting can only be
learnt at the conductor's desk. On the continent there are
many small posts at opera-houses and in concert-rooms
through which a young man can gradually rise to the front
rank, and obtain an important post as Kapellmeister. In
England there are no such means of learning the art, and
hardly any appointments to be gained at the end.

There are, however, signs of improvement. The Scottish
Orchestra, for instance, is doing splendid work in the north

under the conductorship of Dr. Cowen who is also conductor
to the Philharmonic Society in London: at Bournemouth,
Mr. Dan Godfrey has developed the municipal 'Town Band'
into a first class concert orchestra, where, every year, all the
well-known orchestral music is performed, as well as many
new and little-known compositions by British and foreign
composers. It is to be hoped that the example of Bournemouth will soon be followed, and that every large munici-
pality will support a local orchestra presided over by a
resident conductor.

HYMN TUNES

(Extract from the 'Preface on the Music' to *The English Hymnal*,
1906)

The usual argument in favour of bad music is that fine
tunes are doubtless 'musically correct' but that the people
want 'something simple.' Now the expression 'musically
correct' has no meaning; the only 'correct' music is that
which is beautiful and noble. As for simplicity, what could
be simpler than 'St Anne' or 'The Old Hundredth', and what
could be finer?

It is indeed a moral rather than a musical issue. No doubt
it requires a certain effort to tune oneself to the moral
atmosphere implied by a fine melody; and it is far easier to
dwell in the miasma of the languishing and sentimental
hymn tunes which disfigure our services. Such poverty of
heart may not be uncommon, but at least it should not be
encouraged by those who direct the services of the Church;
it ought no longer to be true anywhere that the most
exalted moments of the church-goer's week are associated
with music that would not be tolerated at any place of
secular entertainment.

There are, however, many who recognize this bad state
of things, but are timid about removing old favourites.
Those who have this fear should remember that most of our

'old favourites' are of very recent growth, dating at the earliest from the year 1861—a very short life for a hymn tune; also that it does not take more than a couple of years to make a tune which congregations like into an 'old favourite'; and furthermore that it is not by any means necessarily bad music which is popular. The average congregation likes a fine melody when it can get it, but it is apt to be undiscriminating, and will often take to bad melody when good is not forthcoming. Is it not worth while making a vigorous effort today for the sake of establishing a good tradition? Especially should this be the case with children's hymns. Children at all events have no old association with any particular tune, and incalculable good or harm may be done by the music which they sing in their most impressionable years. A tune has no more right to be dull than to be demoralizing.

When in 1904 Percy Dearmer had asked Vaughan Williams to be the Music Editor of the proposed *English Hymnal,* he said that the work would probably take two months, and that each of the founders would put down five pounds for out-of-pocket expenses. In fact the work took two years and the clerical expenses of the musical side of it alone cost two hundred and fifty pounds. The book was published in 1906, and in a broadcast to celebrate its fiftieth year Vaughan Williams said:

I decided, if I was to do the book at all I must be thorough, adventurous, and honest. . . . As regards honesty: the actual origin of the tune must be stated, and any alteration duly noted. But this does not mean that the original version must necessarily be adhered to. I always tried to find what I believed to be the best version. . . . Cecil Sharp had just made his epoch-making discovery of the beautiful melody hidden in the countryside: why should we not enter into our inheritance in the church as well as the concert room?

So you will find a lot of folk-songs in *The English Hym-nal*. . . . Our first territory to explore was of course the English and Scottish sixteenth and seventeenth-century psalters, many fine tunes out of which had been neglected in modern hymnals. In these tunes I restored what the Scots call the gathering note and in England we designate more pompously, the long initial. I explored particularly Wither's *Hymns and Songs of the Church* because they contained beautiful tunes by Gibbons . . . also Archbishop Parker's *Psalter* containing fine tunes by Tallis. . . . The eighteenth-century psalm books contain many very fine tunes which had been allowed to drop out . . . Then there are the strong Methodist tunes of the eighteenth century. . . . Another fruitful source of good melodies was the Welsh hymnbooks. The German choral was, up to a point, represented in the nineteenth century C. of E. hymnbooks, but often in a distorted form: so far as possible *The English Hymnal* has restored the originals. . . . I intended the music to be congregational, both in matter and manner: the choir and organist acting as leaders. They have their opportunity to show off in other parts of the service but in hymns they must be the servants of the congregation.

III

LETTERS 1906-1919

Letter XIII

Vaughan Williams to Holst
The Warren
Meldreth
Cambs   [1906]

My dear V.

It was nice to open yr parcel and find my initials over your pieces*—I don't know what you owe to me—but I know all I owe to you—if I ever do anything worth doing it will be greatly owing to having such a friend as you 'at my command' as the folk-songs say, always ready to help and advise—and someone whose yea is always yea & nay, nay—which is a quality one really wants in a friend and so seldom gets.

I do thank you from the bottom of me—because I know that you don't do these things unless you mean them.

I've just finished scoring the 2nd movement of the ocean.†

Yrs
RVW

Letter XIV

Vaughan Williams to Holst

[Early 1908]

My Dear V.

Do you really think that because your work‡ has been crowned with the disfavour of Joseph Bennet, that my &

---

*Holst's *Two Songs Without Words* for small orchestra, published 1906, were dedicated to Vaughan Williams.

†*A Sea Symphony*, on which Vaughan Williams worked for about

other people's labours, in scratching out your mistakes is made any the more or less worthwhile?—The point is that it's a big work & naturally anything one does to help on that is not wasted.

I'm sorry (a) that you haven't got £500,
          (b) that you are not promised a performance.
Perhaps these are rather important side issues but they *are* side issues—the real, important thing is that you have *not* been put in the awful position when 'all men speak well of you'—Think, the awful stigma to have gone through life with a prize opera on your back—almost as damning as a mus: doc:

I'm glad on the whole that you are 'highly commended'—because it probably means that *one* judge (perhaps Stanford?—or Percy Pitt?) did really know a good thing when they saw it—and it may be practically useful as far as performance goes.

P. [Plunkett] Greene has written me a very silly letter saying he doesn't like your songs & has sent them back to me—they are at 13 Cheyne Walk.

To return to the opera

I don't know that even my faith in you w^d have been quite strong enough to have stood the shock of approval by J. Bennet.

So after all, at the expense of worldly advantages, you've saved your honour.

Perhaps you think it is too serious a matter to joke about —well, I know it is—but then after all the *most* important thing is that you've written a big work and that you aren't in the awful position of being continually praised by those whose opinions & methods you despise in every way.

                                        Y
                                        RVW

seven years. During this time the title was altered several times and the text was changed, but only in detail.

‡Holst sent in his opera *Sita* for the Ricordi prize in 1908; he failed to win it.

Letter XV

Vaughan Williams to Holst
Hotel de L'Universe et du Portugal
Paris [1908]

Dear V.

What do you say to £50 at Easter (or when you want it)
& £25 more in September*

—It *might* be £50 in September—but I can't be sure yet—
so we mustn't count on it. Now is this enough to do you any
good? If not, say so & we will try & devise something else—
because if we do this job at all we must do it properly.

It is most important—to my mind—that this should be a
real holiday to make up for all your past years of strain. If
you compose during it all the better—but if you have an
idea all the time that you must have something to show
for it—then you will spoil your holiday and effectually
prevent yourself composing. If—even—you only come back
teaching very well it w^d mean that it came easier & left you
more energy for other work.

I think abroad sounds good—but I don't know why it
should be very long abroad—enough to give you a change
and a filip—but we can discuss all this when I come back.

[Later]

Dear V.

This was to have been about Ravel—but I am too sleepy
& I can tell you all about it later—only it is doing me just
the good I hoped it w^d—I go to him 4 or 5 times a week.†

Yr

R V.W

Letter XVI

Vaughan Williams to Holst

[1910?]

Dear V.

Here's to C.M. [*Cloud Messenger*]. I've just been through

---

*Holst had a month's holiday in Algeria as a result of this present.
†Early in 1908 Vaughan Williams stayed in Paris for several months
in order to have lessons from Ravel.

PLATE 5

A walking tour

PLATE 6

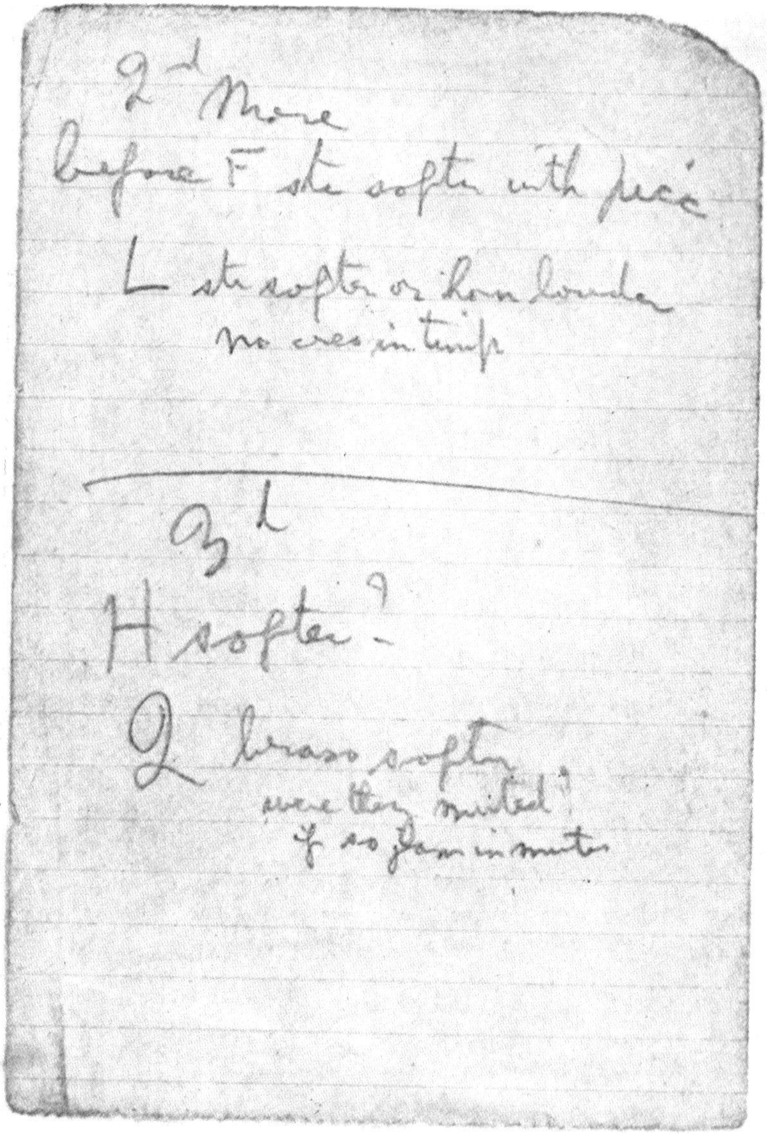

2d Move
before F str softer with picc
L str softer or horn louder
no cres in timp
3d
H softer?
Q brass softer
were they muted?
if so jam in mutes

Facsimile of Holst's notes during a rehearsal of the London Symphony it for the 2ⁿᵈ time (that makes the 4ᵗʰ time altogether) & I like it more each time—most of it is beautiful & there are only one or two places I don't care for which I shall not bother you with as they are merely matters of opinion.

However two general criticisms

(i) Too many steigerungs on a pedal—I should cut out *both* the 'To the Northward' (p. 18) and 'and see' (p. 10 of *your* copy) & keep only the big one before the temple scene which will gain much thereby.

(ii) There's perhaps rather too much wiggling on a chord of the 7th or something else with a persistent figure going. . . . The end good (lots of it A.1.) but rather long: actual last 9 bars I *don't like.*

RVW

Letter XVII

Holst to Vaughan Williams
10 Luxemburg Gardens
Brook Green, W.
Sunday [29 March 1914]

Dear R V W

You have really done it this time. Not only have you reached the heights but you have taken your audience with you. Also you have proved the musical superiority of England to France. I wonder if you realized how futile and tawdry Ravel sounded after your Epilogue.* As a consequence of last Friday I am starting an anti-Gallic League the motto of which shall be 'Poetry not Pedantry'. More when we meet!

I enclose the £30 you so kindly lent me. It has saved the situation very effectively and I am sorry I could not return it before. I believe Coles† has talked to you about his affairs —probably he is right although I feel it is risky.

If you are free, do come a walk next Sunday. The

---

*London Symphony. First performance at Queen's Hall, 27 March 1914. The programme included Ravel's *Valses Nobles et Sentimentales.*
†Cecil Coles, a young composer who was killed in the 1914–18 war.

Masons* have invited me to hear Boughton play his music drama that evening.

I wish I could tell you how I and everyone else was carried away on Friday. However it is probably unnecessary as I expect you know it already.

Yrs Ever
GVH

In the early autumn of 1914 Vaughan Williams enlisted in the R.A.M.C.; he served as a private in the 2/4th Field Ambulance in England, France, and Salonika. In 1917 he returned to England and after training at the R.G.A. Officer Cadet School he served in France as a 2nd Lieutenant. After the Armistice in November 1918 he became Director of Music, First Army B.E.F., based at Valenciennes. He was demobilized in February 1919.

Holst tried to enlist at the beginning of the war but he was rejected as unfit for military service or for any active war work owing to his neuritis and his short sight. He therefore went on with his teaching at St. Paul's Girls' School and at Morley College, holding informal festivals of music every Whitsun at his home in Thaxted.

Towards the end of the war the education department of the Y.M.C.A. appointed him Musical Organizer to the troops in the Near East. He worked in Salonika and Constantinople from November 1918 to June 1919. It was for this appointment that he dropped the 'von' in his name.

Letter XVIII
Vaughan Williams to Holst
Sutton Veney [June 1916]
Dear V.

We are on the eve—all packed & ready—I can't say more —write to me occasionally, my wife will give you the address.†

*Edward Mason gave concerts of British music at the Queen's Hall during the years just before the war.
†The 2/4th Field Ambulance left Salisbury Plain for France on Midsummer Day 1916.

Your letter about Thaxted was splendid—I sometimes feel that the future of musical England rests with you—because every Paulina who goes out, & for the matter of that every Morleyite, will infect 10 others & they in their turn will infect 10 others—I will leave you to make the necessary calculation.

Good luck to you—I feel that perhaps after the war England will be a *better* place for music than before—largely because we shan't be able to buy expensive performers etc. like we did. I wish I c^d have been there—perhaps next Whit:—who knows? I read your letter over & over again, it was so inspiriting—We don't take music as part of our every-day life half enough—I often wish we could all migrate to some small town where there could really be a musical community—London is impossible from that point of view.

Goodbye & good luck

Yrs   RVW

Letter XIX

Vaughan Williams to Holst

[Autumn 1916?]

Dear V

I was most touched by your letter. I've indeed longed to be home in many ways during the last month—but in other ways I should not like to come home for good till everything is over, or in some other normal way.

Remember me to all the Morleyites and wish them good luck from me—& I shall think of all your schoolgirls on All Saints Day.

I sometimes dread coming back to normal life with so many gaps—especially of course George Butterworth—he has left most of his MS to me—& now I hear that Ellis* is killed—out of those 7 who joined up together in August 1914 only 3 are left—I sometimes think now that it is wrong to have made friends with people much younger

*F. B. Ellis, a close friend of George Butterworth's.

than oneself—because soon there will only be the middle aged left—& I have got out of touch with most of my contemporary friends—but then there is always you & thank Heaven we have never got out of touch & I don't see why we ever should.

Goodbye yrs
RVW

Letter XX

Vaughan Williams to Holst

[Summer 1918]

Dear V.

I've not written to you ever since I came out this time (nor for the matter of fact you to me). But I keep posted up in all your doings & I see your letters.

I wonder if you will go to Holland—I sh^d feel more inclined for the naval job myself—but still there is the 3rd alternative I hope, of your stopping at Morley—when all this is over it will I believe the people who've kept the lamp alight who will count as the heroes.

The war has brought me strange jobs—can you imagine me in charge of 200 horses!! That's my job at present—I was dumped down on to it straight away, and before I had time to find out which were horses and which were wagons I found myself in the middle of a retreat—as a matter of fact we had a very easy time over this—only one horse killed so we were lucky.

At present I am down near the sea undergoing a 'gunnery course'—more of a rest than anything else—but it's given me an opportunity of learning something about my gun (among other things.) Having been trained entirely as a 6″ Howitzer man I've been bunged into a 60 p^dr!

I wish I c^d have been at Thaxted—but that will all come after the war—I sh^d be very sorry for you to leave Morley & Thaxted and all that—but it w^d be interesting to see if you have established a tradition & if it will carry on without you.

Let me have a letter when you can. What are you writing?

Yrs
RVW

address 2/Lt RVW R G A
141 Heavy Bty
B E F France

Letter XXI

Holst to *Vaughan Williams*
Y.M.C.A.
British Post Office
Constantinople
April 12 [1919]

Dear R

. . . The enclosed [programme of a concert of British music in Constantinople] was quite a success. . . . Demobilization was in full swing, and between it and flu and malaria I had a different orchestra every two days and sometimes almost every two hours. At the end we had to get men from four different units to fill up. Can you guess what that meant in transport?

The Wednesday before, we gave the concert, barring the choral items, at the Church Hall Summerhill. It was packed with a jolly, keen, rowdy audience who hardly breathed during the music, who kindly laughed noisily at all my jokes (I spouted mildly before each item) and then bellowed and stamped by way of applause.

It was so good that I feared that the big concert would fall flat—which it didn't.

A big uninvited audience came to both full rehearsals.

I believe one of the big sights was the audience that did *not* get into the concert because there was no room left— red-hatted officers amongst them. Anyhow I've never seen such a crowd as the one that did get in.

They stood 4 to 6 deep all round the seats, they over-flowed into the orchestra, and others got round to the back

of the choir and into the green room. Then of course we had
a big crowd outside. And the whole thing had to be repeated
the following night 'to prevent a free fight' as I was told.

At last my books and music have arrived so that life is
easier than at Salonica. They were sent out in October and
arrived in March.

How are things with you?

Yours Ever
Gustav

IV

HOLST'S LECTURE NOTES

ENGLAND & HER MUSIC

THESE notes formed the basis of several talks Holst gave during the 1920s to his pupils at Morley College and St. Paul's Girls' School, and to the students of Reading and Liverpool Universities. The short, bare statements were only meant to remind him of what he wanted to say, but their directness is characteristic.

SOME years ago a Frenchman said: 'The English love music, but they can do without it.' This is probably the best answer we have had to that old query: 'Are we a musical nation?'. *The mere question suggests doubt.*

No question and no doubt about literature—our national form of art.

Compare the place occupied in our national life by the two.

English literature: a steady flame shining through centuries.

English music: a fitful flare—sometimes an explosion of musical energy followed by a long period of darkness. ('They can do without it.') At the next explosion English musicians have either forgotten their forefathers or they disapprove of them.

A fitting epitaph to nearly every great English composer: 'Fifty years after his death English music was as if he had never existed.'

The epitaph applies to the complete Tudor tradition as well as to each individual composer of Elizabeth's reign.

Milton calls Henry Lawes 'the first to wed music and the English language.' Yet Milton's father was a Tudor composer—a contemporary of Dowland, one of the world's greatest song writers.

The bleakest period of English music lasted for nearly 200 years after Purcell's death in 1695. By the beginning of the 19th century our national music had fallen into a not undeserved contempt. Music became a foreign language. This attitude lasted till nearly 1900. It was understood that if you were a good musician you must be a foreigner. And if you were a foreign musician it followed that you must be a better one than an English one. And although things are less silly than they were in the 19th century they are bad enough. Any experienced concert-giver knows that certain English audiences will prefer foreign music and musicians as such to native ones. Others—for instance the Proms audience—give us a chance.

1880 is usually given as the date of the 'modern Renaissance' in English music. For me it began about 20 years later when I first knew Elgar's Enigma Variations. I felt that here was music the like of which had not appeared in this country since Purcell's death.

And 30 years' experience has deepened my conviction that today we are having another rebirth of English music. I believe that every department of music in England is in a better condition now than it was when I was a boy.

Choral music The best Victorian choirs sang certain things superbly. Today's best choirs aim at being able to interpret *anything*.

Orchestral playing . . . surely better than in 1893. (Lack of rehearsal gives greater alertness and brilliance [but also] frequent lack of finish. Both often increased by no permanent conductor.)

Solo singing English singers today sing the English language.

Musical critics criticize more today—formerly they hedged.

Audiences for good music infinitely larger.

Perhaps greatest change has been in musical *education*.

. . . (Of course every change brings fresh dangers. Neither art nor life should be fool-proof.)

In every form of music there is more breadth of aim, more keenness for fresh knowledge whether of old or new music, less complacency, more real love for the sound of good music and less reverence for names.

But no abuse of Victorian musicians—If we are better— which some deny—it is because they taught us so well. And if we are better we are only *beginning* to be better. We have an abiding joy in music: we need to cultivate an abiding sensitiveness to beauty on the part of English composers, English performers, and English audiences.

Chief reason for optimism—the healthy impatience everywhere—the desire for something better and something more. In 1893 England had no money to spare for orchestras (outside Manchester). Since the War people are demanding them—and getting them sometimes.

'We are not really musical here,' said everywhere. Nearly always flatly contradicted by facts—as in Liverpool's concert list. If Liverpool people go to all these Liverpool concerts they must have some feeling for music. (Average programmes very good.)

Of course all this might be more organized both in Liverpool and in England. But is organization in art really good in itself? Organization gets very near standardization at times. *As things are* we need more organization. But the need is temporary and too much would be worse than too little.

Organization should be in the direction of raising the standard of finished performance.

I have suggested that music in England is a tale of ups and downs. If we are going up now can we avoid another 'down'? Is it merely another fitful flare, to be followed by another period of darkness? Some critics have assured us that the darkness is already setting in. I believe they are mistaken. And I believe that it is *possible* that our light may shine as steadily henceforth in music as in literature.

H.R.—E

Something is happening in England in the 20th century that has never happened before. For the first time in the history of English music we are trying to learn to honour and appreciate our forefathers.

We know our national folk-songs and dances. (I knew none till I was over 25.)

Less than 12 years ago we were able for the first time to know all the Tudor madrigals.

Less than 12 years ago we *began* to learn the complete Tudor sacred music.

I learnt as a boy that Campian and Dowland were poets. We are learning that they were great song writers— Dowland now ranks with Schubert.

This unearthing of musical treasures is still going on. It is a movement of young enthusiasts as well as learned antiquarians.

We are laying a sure foundation of our national art.

We are entering into our national musical heritage.

MY FAVOURITE TUDOR COMPOSER

(From an article in *The Midland Musician*, January 1926)

Thomas Weelkes is my favourite Tudor composer because I get more enjoyment and less disappointment from his music than I do from that of any of his contemporaries.

'Less disappointment' is important when we compare him—as we can hardly avoid doing—with William Byrd. No artist is always at his very best. Byrd's misfortune is that when he is not first-rate he is so rarely second-rate—he drops to third or fourth-rate and gives us music that might have been written by anyone.

Weelkes, on the other hand, rarely descends below his second rate. All his music is Weelkes and Weelkes is in all his music. This is probably due to the variety of his work. No one in any age or country has expressed so many different ideas and moods in pure choral music; and—being, like Byrd, a master of choral writing—he always expresses them beautifully and well.

It is characteristic of Weelkes that a volume of his shorter choral works should be entitled *Airs or Fantastic Spirits*. The spirit of fantasy, which was to disappear from choral music less than a hundred years after his death, runs through all his work and is only absent when the subject forbids its presence. Weelkes shows this fantastic spirit in his choice of words. Take some of the titles of his madrigals: 'Mars in a Fury'; 'Thule, the period of Cosmography'; 'The Ape, the Monkey and Baboon'; 'Come Sirrah Jack Ho! fill some Tobacco'; 'Four Arms, Two Necks, One Wreathing'; 'As Deadly Serpents'; 'Like two Proud Armies marching in the Field.' You will not find the like among Byrd's and Palestrina's works. His music grows out of these words. Nothing is so certain with Weelkes as the unexpected.

He and Thomas Morley were the two great writers of *ballets*—short quick part-songs, harmonic rather than contrapuntal in character, each half-verse of which ended in a 'Fa la la!' Weelkes wrote perfect examples of the ordinary ballet such as 'Sing we at pleasure' and 'To shorten Winter's Sadness,' but it is interesting to notice how he introduced variety into a somewhat square form.

(1)—Variety of Rhythm. In 'Hark all ye lovely Saints' he gives us dazzling contrasts of measures of two and three beats—the type of music that England is supposed by some to have first learned from Russia in the twentieth century.

(2)—Variety of Mood. The alternation of joy and sorrow is a favourite one of Weelkes, as in 'Phyllis, go take thy pleasure' and 'My tears do not avail me.'

(3)—In some ballets the style is so elaborate that one hardly knows whether the work in question is a ballet or a madrigal. Such, for instance, are 'On the plains, Fairy trains'; 'Say, Dainty Dames'; and 'Sing, Shepherds, after me.' This is true of certain works of other Tudor composers, but hardly to the same degree. Weelkes is the great example of all that distinguishes the English sixteenth-century composers from their Italian contemporaries.

To find Weelkes in his most fantastic mood one must go to such things as 'Thule, the period of Cosmography' and 'The Andalusian Merchant' who returns home 'laden with cochineal and china dishes.' But the spirit of fantasy was so strong in him that it is seen and felt equally well when Weelkes treats more conventional subjects, such as his contribution to *The Triumphs of Oriana* ('As Vesta was from Latmos Hill descending'); or 'As wanton Birds' and 'Sweetheart, Arise.' One feels its influence even in his sad music. In the latter he brings a fresh element into his work —that of chromatic harmony. 'Cease Sorrow', 'O Care, thou wilt dispatch me,' and 'Hence Care,' are well known to scholars: let us hope they soon will be equally known by singers and listeners.

The startling originality of some of the harmonic progressions is only equalled by the skilful easiness of the writing. Together with the three madrigals last named one must mention the three beautiful but little-known Elegies, 'Cease now delight'; 'Noel, adieu'; and 'Death hath deprived me.'

Until recently we have always looked on Weelkes as a secular composer, and even now we know very little of his sacred music; but that is as characteristic and as beautiful as his madrigals. Take the six-part motet 'Hosanna to the Son of David.' One remembers the well-known setting of the same words by Orlando Gibbons, with its joyous brilliancy, its elaborate interweaving of parts. How has it been set by Weelkes, the 'Fantastic Spirit,' the master of counterpoint, of chromatic harmony, of complicated rhythms? As usual, Weelkes gives us the unexpected. His motet is *stern*! Coming to it after that of Gibbons is like entering St. Bartholomew's, Smithfield, after leaving King's College Chapel, Cambridge. And while Gibbons, Bach, and all other contrapuntal composers seize on the word 'Hosanna' to display all possible wealth of brilliant intricacy of part-writing, Weelkes stays the flow of his counterpoint at the word and blends his voices into one tremendous Shout! Weelkes is the true English artist. He is an individualist as opposed to the Latin artist who tends to be a member of a school, and as opposed to the inartistic Englishman whose thinking and feeling are arranged for him by convention. There is nothing to suggest that Weelkes hated conventionality. It simply did not exist for him. When his treatment of a subject happened to coincide with the convention of the day, it just coincided, and there is only the superb craftsmanship to show us which is his work. In everything he wrote, this craftsmanship enabled him to express all he felt in his own inimitable manner, whether simply or with elaboration, whether in a style that was to vanish from the earth after his day, or in a style similar to that which most people regard as belonging to the twentieth century.

Such is Weelkes. It is good to know him, and better still, to hear his music. To sing it is best of all.

SAMUEL WESLEY

(From a lecture, 1927)

I once ventured to suggest that centenaries are desirable institutions in this country: that 'England needs one per week.'

'What and how much does he mean to us?' It is good to ask this question once in a hundred years about any man whose name has been handed down to us as worthy of honour.

An artist may win our gratitude for the joy he gives us even if he is not one of the great ones. I am grateful to many—Grieg, Johann Strauss, Bizet, and others—besides Wesley and Pearsall. I bracket these last together because they were two brilliant exceptions to a musically dull period in England. As we look back on them they appear as two 'lesser lights ruling the night.'

As opposed to the 'night' of 1800, we are all agreed that the Tudor period was brilliant 'day,' and most authorities maintain that we are having another day now. The alternation of light and darkness, or of brilliance and dullness, is typical of the long history of English music. Another characteristic is the prevalence of good choral singing and good choral writing. We always write well for the chorus although the music itself may be of poor quality.

Wesley, in his best choral works, gives us the abounding vitality of a man 'rejoicing in the strength of his own works.' In 'Sing aloud with gladness' he resembles a speaker who is so carried away by his subject he can talk of nothing else, neither can he stop. This continual harping on one theme is caused by undisciplined strength rather than weakness. But it is a fault all the same. The work is not perfect [but] it certainly is remarkable. It represents a breaking away from a tradition that was becoming too facile. It is a work of art arising from inspiration and the joy of creation as opposed to standardized mass production. Standardized mass production may be a new blessing in motor cars. It is an ancient curse in art and all other mental activity.

In 'Sing aloud' Wesley deserves our admiration and respect as a pioneer, just as Berlioz does in some of his earlier and less successful works.

'In exitu Israel' is a great work, great in conception, in wealth of melody, in the amazing interweaving of these melodies, and, above all, in its abounding vitality which continues almost to the last note.

A great work is not necessarily a perfect one. I call Debussy's *L'Après-Midi* a perfect work: Schubert's symphony in C is to me a great work, and it remains great in my mind although I recognize the truth of certain criticisms of it.

One way of honouring Wesley is to put him with the best and criticize him accordingly. About seventy per cent of his music is still in manuscript. I trust that no one will do him the injustice of printing all he ever wrote. The fact that he wrote much dull, conventional music is unimportant. Every artist should be judged by his best work. And Wesley's best work is superb.

TWO FRAGMENTS ON MUSICAL EDUCATION

1. From a talk on *Certain Possibilities of the School Orchestra*. (Reported in *The Music Student*, February 1916)

'Amateur' should not be a term of reproach. We are training 'amateurs' in our ordinary school work. Budding professionals are rare, and will be none the worse for a little amateur training.

An amateur orchestra isn't meant to be listened to. Over the door of every amateur concert a notice should be written: 'Audience only admitted at owner's risk; the company does not hold itself responsible for any damage incurred.'

Never do anything because someone else does; also beware of giving music to an orchestra because it will do them good (like medicine).

You are there to make them love music, and the first and obvious thing to do is to give them music you like yourself.

Then as to arranging (or perhaps one should say re-arranging) music for the orchestra. Don't be afraid of altering notes—music is *sound*, and it is this that matters, not the printed notes.

2. Headings for a discussion with Sir Hugh Allen on the training of music students.

(From an undated notebook; probably 1918)

Allen.

amateur v. prof.

  ,,   basis   ,,

emotion—love of m—hard work—but no critical power

all training makes it sham science

worship of hard work

Butler 'never learn anything'* etc
writing not quickly but well
harmony: cut everything beyond [illegible figure]
counterpoint: Weelkes Byrd or——?
    sing it first
only use beautiful tunes
beauty and style from the first
each student should sing in choir
    exams=drugs

    *Never learn anything until the not knowing it has come to be a
nuisance to you.

                          From *The Notebooks of Samuel Butler*.

V

LETTERS 1922-1928

Letter XXII

Holst to Vaughan Williams

Friday. [1922]

Vaughan Williams had sent Holst his *Mass in
G minor* which was dedicated to him and his
Whitsuntide Singers.

Dear R

It arrived on Wednesday but I only got *It* yesterday and
shall not be able to look at *It* properly until tomorrow
morning.

. . . . How on earth Morleyites are ever going to learn the
Mass I don't know. It is quite beyond us but still further
beyond us is the idea that we are not going to do it. I've
suggested that they buy copies now and then when we meet
in September I'll sack anyone who does not know it by
heart!

I'm thinking that the best plan for next season will be to
chuck J S B and at the first concert do a little Byrd and a
little R V W—then at the summer concert do a little Byrd
and a lot of R V W.

We are all tremendously proud of the dedication.

Yrs Ever

G

Letter XXIII

Holst to Vaughan Williams

[Dec: 1923?]

Dear R

I have nothing more to say so I will merely give you the
recapitulation section in close stretto.

1) Its what Ive been waiting for for 47½ years.*
2) The performance was so full of You—even apart from the places I cribbed from you years ago.
3) Are you willing to sign a contract to conduct every first performance I get during the next 10 years or so?
4) You are teaching those people to sing!
5) Pray accept my Blessing

Y
G

Letter XXIV

Vaughan Williams to Holst
Dec 31. [1923]
N.B. This is not a new years letter
tho' it sounds like it.

Dear Gustav

I won't have you talking about 'bother'—there is no necessity for you and me to talk about such things—but in this case I am *going* to say what a wonderful experience it was for me & all of us learning your wonderful music—which got better & better as we went on. It was a tussle I admit—but from the first they loved it—& I know of no other work which I shd have dared to make a choir slog so at—There—you must bear with me so far.

. . . Today I go to Middlesboro' for an Eisteddfoddd(dd)

Yrs
RVW

Letter XXV

Vaughan Williams to Holst
The first London performance of Holst's *Choral*
Symphony was given by the Royal Philharmonic
Society at the Queen's Hall on 29 October 1925.
Undated: no address. [1925]

Dear Gustav

I feel I want to write & put down (chiefly for my own benefit) why I felt vaguely disappointed after the Phil (so

*On 19 December 1923 the Bach Choir, conducted by Vaughan Williams, gave the first London performance of Holst's *Ode to Death*. It was given twice in the programme.

you need not read this.) Not perhaps disappointed—I felt cold admiration—but did not want to get up & embrace everyone & then get drunk like I did after the H of J [Hymn of Jesus]. I think it is only because it *is* a new work & I am more slowly moving than I used to be & it's got to soak in.

But first I want to set down the bits where I was all there, viz. the opening (a great surprize to me)
    Dorothy [Silk]'s first solo,
    the orchestral end of the scherzo,
    the two lovely tunes in the Finale.
Then again I've come to the conclusion that the Leeds Chorus *CANNOT SING*—the Bacchus Chorus sounded like an Oratorio.

As to the Grecian Urn it was *pattered* not sung—No phrasing & no legato—If only the B.C. [Bach Choir] c^d sing in tune or Morley had any tenors we c^d show them how to do it.

In the scherzo they made the words sound so *common.*

I couldn't bear to think that I was going to 'drift apart' from you musically speaking. (If I do, who shall I have to crib from?)—I don't believe it is so—so I shall live in faith till I have heard it again several times & then I shall find out what a bloody fool I was not to see it all first time.

Forgive me this rigmarole—but I wanted to get it off my chest.

Yrs
RVW

Letter XXVI

Holst to Vaughan Williams
[In reply to the previous letter]
St Paul's Girls' School
Brook Green, Hammersmith, W.6.
Nov 11 [1925]

Dear R

It was good to read and re-read your letter today. One of the reasons for its goodness being that it contains much that I felt but failed to get into words about 'Flos' [Campi].

The only point in which I differ from you is about the fear of drifting apart musically or in any other way. I expect it is the result of my old flair for Hindu philosophy and it is difficult to put simply.

It concerns the difference between life and death which means that occasionally drifting is necessary to keep our stock fresh and sweet. It also means a lot more but that's enough for one go.

Of course there's another side and about this I'm absolutely in the dark. I mean the real value of either Flos [Campi], the K S [Holst's Choral, i.e. Keats Symphony] Beethoven's 9th or anything else—barring things like the B minor. During the last two years I have learnt that I don't know good music from bad, or rather, good from less good.

And I'm not at all sure that the K S is good at all. Just at present I believe I like it which is more than I can say about most of my things. I'm quite sure that I like the Mass and P.S. [Pastoral Symphony] best of all your things. I couldn't get hold of Flos a bit and was therefore disappointed with it and me. But I'm not disappointed in Flos's composer, because he has not repeated himself. Therefore it is probably either an improvement or something that will lead to one. Which seems identical with your feelings about the K S.

I am now longing to apologize for all this rigmarole but I see you call your letter one and if getting all this off my chest gives you a quarter of the pleasure that your letter gave me it will have been well worth writing.

I was very sorry to miss the violin concerto.* So far I've only heard Vally [Lasker]'s account which was glowing. She also surprised herself by liking van Dieren.

                                            Yr

                                              G

P.S. I am seriously contemplating giving up all lecturing and conducting after this season. I've spouted and waggled quite enough!

*Vaughan Williams's *Concerto Accademico* had its first performance at the Queen's Hall on 10 October 1925.

PLATE 7

Facsimile of a sketch for Vaughan Williams's Fourth Symphony

PLATE 8

Facsimile of Holst's earliest fragments for Egdon Heath

Letter XXVII

Holst to Vaughan Williams
St. Paul's
Thursday
[May or June 1926]

Dear R

. . . Your letter acted as a much needed tonic and made me do some hard thinking while walking yesterday.

. . . I find that I am a hopeless half-hogger and am prepared to sit on the fence as long as possible, partly through laziness and through force of habit, but chiefly through discovering that if I am a fool in music I am the damndest of damned fools in everything else. Or to put it in other words, I still believe in the Hindu doctrine of Dharma, which is one's path in life. If one is lucky (or maybe unlucky—it doesn't matter) to have a clearly appointed path to which one comes naturally whereas any other one is an unsuccessful effort, one ought to stick to the former. And I am oriental enough to believe in doing so without worrying about the 'fruits of action', that is, success or otherwise. It applies to certain elementary school teachers I have met as well as to Bach. Of course in an emergency one has to throw all this overboard but I fear I only do so at the last moment. And if I don't—if I try and think things out carefully and calmly—I am always wrong. This has happened so often that I am convinced that Dharma is the only thing for me.

This is all first person singular but that cannot be helped. I suppose it is really a confession.

However that may be, it was a great joy to read and re-read your letter. I am free each evening except next Monday if you feel like a meal and a talk. Unless I hear to the contrary I shall conclude that Sancta Civ.* is June 10 and B minor the 11th.

Yrs Ever

G

*The first London performance of Vaughan Williams's cantata *Sancta Civitas* was given by the Bach Choir on 9 June 1926.

Letter XXVIII

Vaughan Williams to Holst

13 Cheyne Walk S.W.3.

Feb 25 [1928]

Dear Gustav

I've come to the conclusion that E.H. ['Egdon Heath']
is beautiful—bless you therefore

Yrs

RVW

As a postscript to this letter it is interesting to read a paragraph
from Vaughan Williams's article in the summer number of the
Royal College of Music Magazine, 1934, which was devoted to
the memory of Holst:

'I remember once discussing Egdon Heath with him. I suggested that the very clearness of the melodic outlines of the piece
were at variance with its atmospheric nature: indeed that less
robust melody would have been more successful in impression-
istic suggestion. Holst, on that occasion, lived up to his own maxim
"always ask for advice but never take it." I am glad that he did
so, for I now see that a less clear melody would have softened and
thereby impaired the bleak grandeur of its outline.'

Letter XXIX

Vaughan Williams to Holst

Eversleigh Court
105/109 Cromwell Road
South Kensington.

[?1928]

Dear Gustav

This is splendid news. I shall think of you at S.P.G.S.
on Wed.

I wish you could have been there on Sunday and Wed:
Its been one of the joys of my life rehearsing with that
orchestra: their wonderful responsiveness & flexibility
(when you say 'pp please' they *play* pp—shades of the
L.S.O.!) & they know what you want before you know it
yourself.

I had 3 rehearsals and really didn't know what to do with them. The 1st one (thank heaven) was only supposed to be two hours, but I gave out $\frac{1}{2}$ hr before time & the final one nearly an hour before time. I told them I wished I could have kept them at it merely for the pleasure of hearing them play. As a matter of fact the 1st movement of the P.S. [Pastoral Symphony] did not seem to me to go as well as sometimes—entirely my fault because I could not get going *myself* & exaggerated, I think, a bit to make up for it. My greatest triumph was when Robert Murchie said 'We've had a very enjoyable evening'! We trotted out the old '4 Hymns' once again—I quite liked them.

Dorothy [Silk] sang them extremely well though a little nervous.

Goodbye and Welcome home

Yrs RVW

VI

HOLST'S LECTURE AT YALE ON THE TEACHING OF ART, 1929

[In 1924 Holst had been given the Howland Memorial Prize by Yale University, a medal awarded to 'a citizen of any country in recognition of some marked distinction in the field of literature or the fine arts'.]

A T last I have an opportunity of thanking this university for the honour she did me in presenting me with the Howland prize. This, in itself, was sufficient cause for gratitude. But this feeling of gratitude was rendered greater when I read the list of previous prize winners.

I felt then that I had received the greatest honour this world can give—the company of honourable men.

In talking of the Teaching of Art I shall chiefly use illustrations from my own art, music.

But I trust that most of what I have to say may be of interest to all of you as it applies to every kind of art, not only the 'Fine' ones, and to teaching in general.

Most people who have mastered any form of intellectual activity either are, have been, or are in danger of becoming teachers even for a short time.

It is a fate that few escape.

At the same time it is noticeable that the teacher is an object of derision amongst many writers of today.

He is held up as being too pedantic in trifles and, above all, too fond of giving good advice.

Personally I think this applies still more to the critics of teachers—people who have never done a day's teaching in their lives and therefore are able to criticize us more freely.

All the same it is often quite true of many of us.

It is true of me at this moment. I am going to indulge in advice-giving now.

I suggest that teachers should be good trades-unionists and in such matters as correcting others and giving good advice we should not work overtime without extra pay.

A second reason for our unpopularity is summed up in a saying of George Bernard Shaw:

'Those who can, do: those who can't, teach.'

As a mere statement of facts this is fairly accurate.

In the musical profession nearly everyone has to teach. The reason is an economic one—there is a larger demand for teachers than for singers and players.

That remark of Shaw is not *essentially* true.

Teaching is not an alternative to doing.

Teaching *is* doing. Teaching is an art.

'Those who can, do.' Those who teach also 'do'.

My subject today is this 'doing' in its relation to the training of artists.

In the teaching of art we aim at the production of artists, of exceptional people, of aristocrats, in whatever department of life they may happen to be, whether builders of cathedrals or good cooks in village inns.

The best definition of what I call an aristocrat is Gilbert Murray's: 'Every man who counts is a child of a tradition and a rebel from it.'

The production of such a man is the aim of the teaching of art.

If we are teachers our first duty is to make our pupil a child of a tradition.

We can only do that if we are ourselves its children. Not merely students but children, steeped in the love of our tradition—that unconscious love that children possess and which is the most contagious emotion in the world.

Our influence on our pupil is assured if we have this.

This influence will be first directed towards developing technical power in the pupil.

H.R.—F

By technique I mean the means by which you express yourself.

And the method of acquiring technique is, for nearly all of us, Hard Work.

People like Mozart, in whom all necessary technique seems to have been born, are too rare to form the basis of an argument.

Of course ideas on hard work vary from time to time.

About a hundred years ago a father brought his six-year-old son to a famous violinist for advice.

The answer was something like this:

'If you want your son to become a violinist make him practise ten hours a day from now until he is twenty-one.'

Today, if a father tried such a plan on a six-year-old boy, he would probably find himself in the police court.

Nowadays the danger is in the other extreme.

In musical circles, a few years ago, we were told: 'We cannot make all our children good singers and players, therefore let us make them good listeners.'

I agree, on condition that we remember that the surest way of becoming a good listener is to first try and sing or play.

For those who are working at technique, some sort of what is called 'Musical Appreciation' is excellent. And in nearly every case the modern systematic system of teaching it is the best.

But I earnestly plead that in all cases it should be coupled with practical experience in making music.

And if there is not time for both theory and practice, let us have practice only.

Using the word in the non-technical sense, appreciation always accompanies genuine technical work, however slight, whether in music or in any other art.

Years ago I cycled with a friend to a famous cathedral.

On arrival I merely wandered about, vaguely trying to impress various details on my mind. My friend spent the whole day in sketching. The sketches were not remarkable and the artist had no illusions about them. But there was no doubt as to which of us two had best realized the beauty of the cathedral.

I have said that the first aim of the teacher should be to make the pupil a child of a tradition.

It must be a living tradition—one of great art and great men.

Such things as standard textbooks and technical exercises must never usurp the place of a living tradition.

But they must not be ignored even if their place be a lower one.

The practice of technical exercises and the learning of textbooks are short cuts.

As someone said the other day: 'The best technique is the laziest way of doing anything.'

It is the best means to an end.

Here, as everywhere else, we are sometimes apt to mistake the means for the end.

That is why I insisted that the teacher must be the child, and the loving child, of a tradition.

And now I am going to use a word that is so often misapplied that I must dwell on its real meaning for a moment.

That word is Stimulant.

To most of us it suggests whisky. But I have been assured on excellent authority that alcohol is not a real stimulant.

In order to be quite sure of my ground I consulted a doctor friend who kindly gave me the following definition.

'A Stimulant is an agent to arouse the nervous system to greater exhibition of energy.

'A true Stimulant imparts no power. It compels brain, muscle, or other part of the organism, to liberate stored-up energy.

'It is on account of this power to exhaust energy that a *large* dose of stimulant produces the same effect as a narcotic.

'It tends to produce narcotism or paralysis.'

As an example of a real Stimulant my friend mentioned

Cold—something natural, inevitable to most of mankind, and moreover, something beneficial.

Bearing this in mind, I ask you to go through my friend's definition again, substituting the word 'Examination' for 'Stimulant'.

I would no more think of condemning examinations and competitions than I would think of condemning cold weather.

It would be almost as futile and quite as silly.

But, just as hard work was, in former generations, sometimes considered as an end in itself and not a means: just as today a few people dream glibly of substituting talking about art for making art and therefore bring the excellent idea of Musical Appreciation into contempt; so, occasionally, one comes upon a piano student whose idea of musical life is just one examination after another; or else a choir, the members of which have lost all feeling for music as music and are only interested in the number of marks they may or may not gain in their competition.

A feeling for music is inherent in nearly all of us, but in the vast majority it is a delicate plant and one that is easily crushed out of existence by that vigorous weed, pot-hunting.

Once again, it is only the over indulgence in this natural, inevitable and beneficial stimulant that is to be deplored.

The Competitive Musical Festivals have been some of the greatest boons in musical education in Great Britain— boons that are still increasing in virtue as well as in mere size.

In every Festival I have attended, the aim seemed to be music first and last. In most cases competitors have been animated by the same spirit.

The stimulation of occasional examinations or other tests and the short cuts in technical training are only two of the many tools which the teacher will use in order to fulfil the first part of Gilbert Murray's definition and make the pupil a child of a tradition.

The teacher being one already, there will grow up

between them that beautiful comradeship which is the great reward of teaching.

We read of painters in former ages whose pupils actually worked in their masters' studios.

What a perfect way of learning art! Imagine the joy of watching a great master of painting at work: and the even greater joy of being allowed to finish a background for him!

But this comradeship of master and pupil has its dangers.

The teacher may consciously or unconsciously influence his pupil too much or for too long.

We must remember the last words in Gilbert Murray's dictum:

'Every man who counts is a child of a tradition and a rebel from it.'

The civilized world is crowded with buildings, pictures, poems, novels and musical compositions produced by children of various traditions who never grew to be rebels and who, therefore, do not 'count'.

If we, as teachers, force the characters of our pupils into a mould or allow them to drift there, we are not artists but experts in standardized mass-production.

I have been told that standardized mass-production is excellent for motor-cars: it is sometimes fairly effective for detective-stories. But it is iniquitous for human beings and impossible for art.

A true work of art is imbued with a vitality of its own.

This appears very clearly in the work of novelists and dramatists.

Over and over again writers have told us how their characters grow individualities of their own and often insist on behaving in a way their creator never intended.

A dramatist has assured us that he has no more control over the women in his plays than he has over his wife.

A novelist is said to have shed tears on discovering that his heroine was going to die.

This is being a creative artist—the creator of men and women who live their own lives.

And this should be the ideal of the teacher of art. It will be so if he is an artist in teaching.

A moment will come when he realizes that he has done his share in the work of creating a 'rebel' who will 'count'. The man who spent his life always retouching one picture instead of leaving it for another would not be a real artist but a more or less interesting study in morbid psychology.

The last and hardest duty of a teacher is to make himself unnecessary.

I have tried to prove to you that the teaching of art is, itself, an art.

Nearly everything I have said about the production of an artist would apply equally to the production of a good picture, poem, symphony, dance, dress, or dinner.

All must spring from a tradition and yet bring something fresh to the world if they are to be works of art.

So if 'those who can, do': those who teach also 'do'.

And in conclusion I would like to point out that those who 'do' usually teach as well.

The vast majority of the great artists of the world have been teachers—usually very good ones.

Of course they grumbled when too much time had to be spent in teaching or when their pupils were more stupid than usual. Who wouldn't?

But this is very different from despising teaching *qua* teaching.

By a happy coincidence the first thing I read on my arrival in Yale was an article by Harold Laski on 'The Academic Mind'. In writing about a certain type of fine thinkers he says 'They have to communicate the truth they have found because, like all great artists, they are born teachers; and silence for them, in the realm they deem supremely important, is worse than death.'

As opposed to these, there is the other type of artist who tries to live in a world by himself: one who despises the vulgar herd and only condescends to allow it to share the beauty of his art in the spirit of a despot of the Middle Ages throwing largesse to the mob. Except for invalids, it is fairly safe to say that when this type of artist is considered great he exists only in second-rate novels: when he exists in real life he is himself second-rate.

We who are teachers should hold up our heads more proudly. We are among the lucky ones of the earth.

If we are real artists in teaching we have the greatest joy this world can give—that of creative work.

We have also what I have called the world's greatest honour—the companionship of honourable men and women.

VII

LETTERS 1930-1934

Letter XXX

Vaughan Williams to Holst

The Royal Philharmonic Society's Gold Medal
was presented to Holst after the first performance of his *Double Concerto*, on 3 April 1930.

> The White Gates,
> Westcott Road,
> Dorking.
> [April 4th 1930.]

Dear Gustav,

I was distressed not to see you last night. I know you hate
it all—but we had to tell you in public that we know you
are a great man.

The Lament & Ground are splendid—I'm not *quite* so
sure about the scherzo—and even that boils down to not
being *quite* sure about the 6/8 tune.

> Yrs
> RVW

Letter XXXI

Vaughan Williams to Holst

> The White Gates
> Westcott Road
> Dorking.
> [December 1930]

Dear Gustav

I've never written to you since the great night at
S.P.G.S.*—I somehow thought we should meet and talk it
over.

*On 12 December 1930 Holst's new works, the *Choral Fantasia*,

The Organ Concerto [*Choral Fantasia*] is IT all right,—there is only one place where I have any doubts—& that is —I think—where the chorus first enters in harmony; [it] sounds a little bit respectable & out of the picture—I shd like very much to talk about that place one day. The organ part is magnificent. . . . In the opera [*The Wandering Scholar*] it was interesting to note that the most obvious amateur of your lot (the schoolmaster) was far the most successful because he was thinking of his *words* and his *part* all the time and not worrying about his damned tone. I know the answer to this is that in a larger place he would not be heard. But is there no way of preserving that *natural* singing and yet getting the voice big enough? One thing is that it is *impossible* to get a big tone on English words—& the sooner singing masters recognize this the better—either sing English with a small tone (Plunket Greene) or don't sing English at all (Caruso). . . .

The opera gave me quite a new idea—the *concert opera*: sit round a table *with copies* & sing with a minimum of action (*no costumes*). I thought it was a perfect representation. Do you think there's a *little* bit too much 6/8 in the opera? I wonder if Nigel Playfair would do it at his light opera season. But I dare say you've thought of that. The one thing I can't yet quite get hold of is 'Hammersmith' —but you are (like your daughter) a realist & you are almost unique in that your stuff sounds better when it is played on the instrument it was originally written for.

I want very much to have a lesson on 'Riders'* soon. I've been revising and rough scoring it.

I wrote to E.E. [Edwin Evans] re: Job but have had no answer.

Yrs
RVW.

The Wandering Scholar, and *Hammersmith* were tried over for the first time in his music room at St. Paul's Girls' School.
*Vaughan Williams's opera *Riders to the Sea*.

Letter XXXII
Vaughan Williams to Holst

Vaughan Williams's *Job* was performed on
5 and 6 July 1931 at the Cambridge Theatre
by the Camargo Society.

> The White Gates
> Westcott Road,
> Dorking.
> [July 1931]

Dear Gustav

I never wrote to thank you for holding my hand all those days—it made all the difference. All went very well in the end.

. . . I don't think you know Duncan (percussion)—I know him because he plays timps for me at Dorking. After rehearsal he came up & begged me to put back one of the cymbal smashes which he thought it had been a great mistake of me to leave out. I was so much touched that I said yes—regardless of the result.

Glad I. [Imogen] got such good notices.

> Yrs RVW

Later, Vaughan Williams enlarged on this in the following quotation from 'A Musical Biography' (written for Hubert Foss by Vaughan Williams and reprinted in his *Some Thoughts on Beethoven's Choral Symphony with writings on other musical subjects*, O.U.P. 1953).

I should like to place on record all that he [Holst] did for me when I wrote *Job*. I should be alarmed to say how many 'Field Days' we spent over it. Then he came to all the orchestral rehearsals, including a special journey to Norwich, and finally he insisted on the Camargo Society's performing it. Thus I owe the life of *Job* to Holst. . . . I remember after the first orchestral rehearsal his almost going on his knees to beg me to cut out some of the percussion with which my inferiority complex had led me to overload the score.

Letter XXXIII
Vaughan Williams to Holst

The White Gates
Westcott Road
Dorking
[September, 1931]

Dear Gustav

I played through the fantasia* again yesterday & it is *most* beautiful—I know you don't care, but I just want to tell the press (and especially ****) that they are misbegotten abortions.

Yrs
RVW

Letter XXXIV
Vaughan Williams to Holst

The White Gates
Westcott Road
Dorking
Undated [1931?]

Dear Gustav

I've been going carefully through the Welsh Folksongs.

It's taken me a little time to get accustomed to them.—I think that is inevitable, because when one is in the trade oneself one gets stereotyped ideas as to how these things should be done. But now I am getting to love the ones I *do* like more and more. 'The Dove', 'Nightingale & Linnet'—beautiful, I think the best words, tune & setting is 'Awake awake'. 'Lisa Lan' & 'Green Grass': I somehow feel the setting rather obscures the outlines of the melody. (I don't care for the tune of Green Grass much.) 'Lovers Complaint' I don't somehow like, (dull tune?) but doubtless my opinions will change. . . .

. . . We must meet soon. . . .

Yrs
RVW

*The first performance of Holst's *Choral Fantasia* was given at the Three Choirs Festival, Gloucester Cathedral, on 8 September 1931.

Letter XXXV
>   *Vaughan Williams to Holst*
>   The White Gates
> March 20   Westcott Road
> [1932]   Dorking

Dear Gustav

I got the 'Intercession' (through Nora Day) Thank you so much. I like it as much as when you played it to me which is a lot.

I've not had a letter from you—but then I haven't written one so I don't deserve one. But I'm longing for news. Imogen gave me a wonderful letter to read all about your adventures with the Boston Symphy orch.

Mrs Herbert Jones spent the aft. with us the other day— & we both liked her *enormously*. She just sat in a chair after lunch & sang & talked and told us her whole life history. I've been invited to Gregynnogg(?)—& am ½ inclined to go.

Otherwise I have no particular news except that I've written a magnificat for Astra Desmond to sing at the Worcester festival—& that I miss you very much when I want to know how to compose—in [fact] I didn't realize how much you wrote of my music before.

I wonder how you enjoy being led by the nose by an American agent—an agent of Foss's wrote to me and wanted to lead me round America for several months—but I shied off.

I started this letter some days ago & then something intervened & I broke off. I do want to know how America goes—& *have you time for your own work*—because I believe the change will produce a great new work from you. But perhaps that will come when you get back— 'emotion remembered in tranquillity' etc.

Did I tell you that I am writing a 'Magnificat' for Worcester Fest? The story is as follows:

(a) . . . I wondered if it w^d be possible to lift the words out of the smug atmosphere which has settled down on it from being sung at evening service for so long. (I've tried hard to get the smugness out; I don't know if I have succeeded—I find it awfully hard to eradicate it.)

(b) Last year at Gloucester rehearsals Steuart [Wilson] (I think) said that it was not quite nice that young unmarried women like Elsie Suddaby should always be singing Magnificats—so Astra Desmond who was there said to me 'I'm a married woman with 4 children why don't you write one for me'—So I promised her if ever I wrote one it should be for her.

Come back soon

Yrs
RVW

Letter XXXVI
Holst to Vaughan Williams
[In answer to the previous letter.]

Harvard University
Division of Music
Cambridge, Massachusetts
April 15 [1932]

Dear R

I'm sorry—

a) that I didn't stop to see you at the **** concert the night before I sailed: but I was tired and rather bored:

b) that my boat got in to N Y six hours late so that I could not send a cable to you and Biddy [Helen Bidder] during the Dorking concert as I had meant to:

c) that all the time I have merely thought of all the things I wanted to write to you about instead of doing the job.

And now comes your lovely long letter—many many thanks.

It's grand news about the Magnificat and I hope to see it soon. Steuart's theology sounds a little unorthodox but his commonsense is unquestionable.

I've had a lovely suite of rooms at Eliot House [Harvard] with a good quiet study. So far I've written two more male voice choruses for [Archibald] Davison's choir. How's the New Sym? [No 4.] When I get home in July I want a 2 piano field day of both old and new versions. When do you arrive in the U S A ? How long will you stay? And will you be able to visit Harvard? In that case I'll lend you Davison's front door key. Please tell H P A [Sir Hugh Allen] I'll do the same to him. It's a useful thing to have in this country.

I'm very glad I've made use of Duncan McKenzie (O U P) as an agent. He has been really helpful and I hope you'll at least consider using him. The alternative would be to print 1000 forms—

'Dear Sir or Madame
       I'll see you damned before I'll conduct, lecture, dine, be interviewed, be photographed'—

I forget the others but there are a few left. You'd probably have to accept all the Mus Docs—I've just refused the 2nd in a month.

I've had three new experiences this year.

I Pretending to be a star conductor. You know all about that now. It was wildly exciting and I had a lovely time with the orchestra.

II Pretending to be a University Professor. Which is Rum. My idea of composition is to spoil as much MS paper as possible. But my pupils here would far rather write a thesis on Schönberg's use of the bass clarinet compared with von Webern's: or, better still, talk vaguely about the best method of introducing the second subject in the recapitulation. And some of these boys have really studied hard—if not music, anyhow books on music. Is this University or is it America? I got square with one ultra-modernist, wrong-note merchant by pointing out that I was an old fogey who was only here for two months more and that when I'd gone he could make up for lost time but that until then he'd better humour me and even, occasionally, write a tune. And he answered cordially, 'Sure'!

III On Easter Day, after lecturing on Haydn in Washington the previous day and having a horrid 14 hour journey back at night, they took me to hospital with a duodenal ulcer. And I learnt the real meaning of the phrase 'A Bloody Nuisance'. They reckoned that I lost two quarts. They gave me a) blood transfusion which was invigorating at first but which gave me a high temperature the next day: b) morphia which is altogether delightful: c) five days diet of 'creamed milk' every hour which was infernal.

I had one beautiful experience which was repeated two nights later. I felt I was sinking so low that I couldn't go much further and remain on earth. As I have always expected, it was a lovely feeling although the second time, as it began, I had a vague feeling that I ought to be thinking of my sins. But a much stronger feeling was that there was something more important on hand and that I mustn't waste time. Both times, as soon as I reached the bottom I had one clear, intense and calm feeling—that of overwhelming Gratitude. And the four chief reasons for gratitude were Music, the Cotswolds, R V W and having known the impersonality of orchestral playing.

I was in hospital 16 days and since then have been staying with the Davisons who are dears. Every day I've been getting stronger and walking more. . . .

My movements are uncertain. If the doctor allows I go to conduct at Ann Arbor about May 17 and then on to Vancouver Island after which a holiday in the Rockies and then home.

But I'm not running any risks and if all these nights and meals in trains won't do I'll come back in the middle of June.

Love to Adeline.
Get on with the Symphony

Y^{rs} Ever

Gustav

Letter XXXVII
Vaughan Williams to Holst

Holst had returned to England in June 1932.
He never fully recovered his health and
strength. The following letter was written just
before Vaughan Williams left England to
lecture at Bryn Mawr College, Pennsylvania.

> The White Gates,
> Westcott Road
> Dorking.
> [September 1932]

Dear Gustav

I was v. sorry not to see you. But it was wonderful having
you on Tues: I feel ashamed of myself sometimes letting
you waste all that nervous energy which you ought to be
spending on your own stuff for me—But it's too late to
mend now & I can't get on without you, so that's that.

. . . .

I wish we had more talk about you & what really matters &
not spent so much time over my damned compos: Your
sentence about 'too much alone' puzzles me—but we will
discuss it in Dec.

> Yrs
> RVW

P.S. I send the £5 from my fund for your performances—don't
say it comes from [illegible] or through me if you can help it

> RVW

Letter XXXVIII
Vaughan Williams to Holst

> The White Gates,
> Westcott Road,
> Dorking
> Undated [end of 1932 or beginning of 1933]

Dear Gustav

For our sake you must keep well—but for the sake of

music you must go on writing canons—so try and continue the two.

I like especially Fields of Sorrow & David's Lament—the two big ones I feel I am going to like—but can't vizualize them yet. I liked the old Trio [Terzetto]—but always felt that its being in 3 keys was more seen by the eye than felt by the ear. After all, 'Lovely Venus' depends a lot on the 'natural chord' doesn't it? I don't think I like your notation. After all, key signatures are simply a means of avoiding accidentals—isn't that so? And I believe that on the balance you w^d get fewer accidentals by putting a christian key signature—& not, incidentally, make unhappy people, like me, who try to play them on the pfte, permanently cross-eyed.

Let me hear them soon. We are perhaps coming to London for a week round Feb 1st.

Yrs
RVW

Letter XXXIX

Holst to Vaughan Williams

St Paul's Girls' School
Brook Green
Hammersmith W.6.
Sep 1. [1933]

Dear R

Thanks for letter re the concerto [Vaughan Williams's Piano Concerto]. I can quite believe that a slow pace for the fugue would make a big difference. How I wish I could have heard it. Thanks also for sending Jane [Joseph]'s Wassail.

It is difficult to thank you for last night* because I've said it all before. I went expecting a real treat but I doubt if I've ever been so carried away by it before—which is saying a great deal.

And I'm going to repeat myself—it's the very essence of you.

*Holst had heard Vaughan Williams conduct his *Pastoral Symphony* on 31 August 1933.

H.R.–G

Which is one of the two reasons (the other being that it
is a beautiful work of art) why it is such an important event
in my life.

It was a stroke of either a) genius, or b) unconscious
humour, to do it just after the Hindemith. It reminded me
of the first definite idea of life I learnt while still in my
cradle. Namely, that music is a nice thing.

Yr

G.

Letter XL

Vaughan Williams to Holst

Holst was now in hospital.

The White Gates

Dorking.

[December 1933.]

Dear Gustav

I was so glad of your letter—it is largely good news—but
6 weeks! I must certainly come and see you if it is allowed.

The 'nice' tunes in the Finale [of *Symphony No. 4*]
have already been replaced by better ones (at all events they
are *real* ones). What I mean is that I *knew* the others were
made-up stuff and these are not.

So there we are. . . .

Yrs

RVW.

Letter XLI

Vaughan Williams to Holst

Holst's *Choral Symphony* was broadcast on
11 April 1934.

The White Gates

Westcott Road

Dorking

Friday [13 April 1934].

Dear Gustav

After promising myself all the year that I would attend
every rehearsal of the choral symphony I attended *none*—I

stupidly went in for a little chill & temperature—nothing
bad, but in view of next week & *having* to go to London for
rehearsals twice this week, I thought I must take no risks.
I was never so disgusted in my life. [Our] wireless behaved
pretty well—funnily the scherzo came over best, I thought,
& as far as I can make out they sang that beautifully—& it
was a relief to hear the Urn* [the slow movement] sung by
people who had some idea what the words meant. . . .

By the way, I wish you would consider taking that last
phrase away from the soloist (even Dorothy) and giving it
to say 4 of the chorus (just as you have done [with] one or
two of the other phrases).

As to the tune its self—I *wholly* liked the Urn for the
first time. I'm not sure that it is the Urn—but it's *you*,
which is all I know & all I need to know.

The scherzo is what I always thought it was; you at your
best.

I am not so sure about the finale. I love the big tune, but
some of it seems to be just getting through the words. I
wonder if a cut of one or two of the poets would be possible
or advisable?

Jelly [d'Aranyi] came & rehearsed the Mendelssohn
concerto with my strings yesterday—we had great fun
singing the wind parts as a duet.

Yrs
RVW

*Keats's *Ode on a Grecian Urn.*

VIII

HOLST'S LECTURE ON HAYDN

This is a shortened version of the lecture
Holst gave in the spring of 1932 while he was
teaching at Harvard.

HAYDN was the most fortunate of all great composers. Of course, I do not mean fortunate in the conventional worldly sense—that he was wealthy and led a life of ease. Neither was he fortunate in being specially gifted as a child—he was no prodigy. I call him fortunate because there was a perfect unity between him and his art. His genius was such that any event in his life was either a source of inspiration or else it had no effect on him.

Moreover, he had the good fortune to meet the sort of people and to take part in the sort of events which could help and inspire him as a composer.

Haydn and Mozart had each admired the other's music before their first meeting, which was probably in 1781, when Haydn was forty-nine and Mozart twenty-five. Haydn learned as much from Mozart as the latter did from him, perhaps more. Their love and respect for each other was untouched by the silly cliques that were formed round them. Theirs is probably the most beautiful friendship in the history of art.

Haydn's remark to Mozart's father is well known—'I declare before God, as an honourable man, that your son is the greatest composer of whom I have ever heard.' Less known is the story of Mozart's reply to a critic of a quartet of Haydn. The critic said: 'I should never have written that passage in that way.' Mozart replied: 'Nor I—neither of us would have thought of anything so good!'

This is one of the few irritable remarks of Mozart that

have come down to us—another proof of the warm affection between the two composers.

It is not possible to overrate the importance of Haydn's twenty-nine years of settled life as composer and director of music to Prince Esterhazy, coming, as they did, after ten years of wandering and poverty. Esterhazy was a musical amateur in the highest sense of the word. Haydn in his old age said of him: 'My prince was always satisfied with my work. Not only had I the encouragement of his constant approval, but being at the head of an orchestra entirely under my orders, I was able to make experiments and try effects. Cut off from the rest of the world, I had nothing to worry about and I was compelled to be original.'

A new era of music appears with Haydn—the era of purely instrumental music. The supreme master of the previous age, John Sebastian Bach, died when Haydn was eighteen. The contrast between Bach and Haydn is one of the greatest in musical history. One may call it the contrast between a Protestant church in Leipzig and a South Austrian court. Technically speaking it was the contrast of counterpoint and harmony: of interweaving strands of melodies as opposed to a single melody with an accompaniment: the contrast of Fugue and Sonata (especially sonata form as applied to the string quartet and the orchestra).

Towards the end of Bach's life his style was becoming out of date, as he himself realized. His son, Carl Philipp Emanuel, [who] was one of the founders of the new style, was the composer from whom both Haydn and Mozart learned most. As Mozart said later: 'He is the father of us all.'

Just as Haydn in Count Esterhazy's palace found a patron, an audience, and an orchestra willing and eager to listen to, to play, and to enjoy his music, so in the early sonata he found a form perfectly suited to his nature, and one capable of expansion and variety in the hands of a master. To this form he brought an unceasing flow of melody, and a never-ending variety of characterization, deep emotion as sincere as it is controlled, a sense of humour—and genius. However fully he accepted the position of servant, he was none the less recognized, by others and himself, as master in purely musical problems. To a criticism of his music by the Prince, Haydn answered: 'Sir, this is my business!'

Haydn is the friend of all musicians, whether professional or amateur. Or, to be accurate, he is the friend of all instrumentalists, of orchestral players, and, above all, of string quartet players. A few years ago when I was conducting several amateur orchestras each week I realized that there were two recurring problems in my life. The pleasant one being: 'Which Haydn symphony shall I do next term?' The difficult one being: 'What orchestral work can I do that is not written by Haydn?'

Perhaps he is a greater friend to players than to listeners, because in playing him you get below the surface more inevitably. Some listeners never see beyond the courtly formality which in his music parallels the wig and court dress he invariably wore. And some critics, equally superficial, having in mind Haydn's unquestioning acceptance of his position as servant, have accused him of 'fleeing from life' and apparently taking refuge from it by writing music. This is as intelligent as accusing a scientist who shuts himself up in the laboratory or observatory day and night of 'fleeing' from the life of New York, London, or Paris.

Another obvious quality in Haydn's music is geniality. The superficial listener finds geniality only, and Haydn has been patronized as a sort of kindly uncle with whom it is nice to spend an afternoon when one has no really important matters with which to employ one's mind. Probably it was a writer of this kind who, in a book I read as a boy, called Haydn a 'bourgeois composer'. But if you listen willingly, or, better still, play his music intelligently, you will gradually realize the depth, breadth, and variety of Haydn's music.

His variety of melody is the first thing one learns. Variety is the first quality; depth of emotion is the last and the greatest that one realizes in his music. He does not proclaim his emotions as certain nineteenth-century composers did; but while discussing some theme he will gently unfold its emotional possibilities without losing his courtly manner of addressing you. If any music student wishes for an example of what I mean, I will give a well-known one—the passage before the recapitulation in the first movement of the so-called 'London Symphony'.

A few years ago I had a non-musical experience, the memory of which is, to me, an embodiment of the essence of Haydn at his best. It was an afternoon with Thomas Hardy shortly before his death. There was a wealth of experience of town and country, deep and controlled emotion, wisdom and humour, all clothed in perfect courtesy and kindliness.

But it is impossible to describe Haydn's genius in words. There is nothing in him but music.

Fame did not move him; at the end of his life his public recognition as the world's greatest symphonic writer does not seem to have excited any emotion beyond the pleasant satisfaction that any healthy-minded man would feel; but when in England he had the new musical experience of hearing Handel's oratorios, *then* he was moved profoundly. The result was that at the age of 66, with a long life of strenuous production in other forms behind him, he gave us a choral masterpiece—'The Creation'. It was something new for him. It is pure Haydn for us.

I have said that he is the friend of all musicians. If you desire an introduction to our friend, that can be arranged quite easily. Get a violin and a good teacher, and after a couple of years or so of preliminary work, join an amateur string quartet or orchestra as second violin. I do not say that in doing so you will be in a position to introduce Haydn to an audience. But after, say, ten years of actually playing Haydn and not merely listening to him, still less reading about him, you will know and will love that which is 'all we know' of him and 'all we need to know'.

IX

VAUGHAN WILLIAMS ON
THE COMPOSER IN WARTIME, 1940

The following article is included because of its
bearing on the letters in Chapter III and the
work Holst was doing in similar circumstances
in the 1914–18 war.

WHAT is the composer to do in wartime? There are three
possible answers. Some lucky devils are, I believe, able to go
on with their art as if nothing had happened. To them the
war is merely an irritating intrusion on their spiritual and
therefore their true life. I have known young composers
refer with annoyance to this 'boring war'. Such a phrase as
this, I confess, shocks me, but it set me wondering
what their point of view was and whether it was a possible
one.

Whatever this war is, it is not boring. It may have been
unnecessary, it may be wrong, but it cannot be ignored: it
will affect our lives and those of generations to come. Is it
then not worth while even for the most aloof artist to take
some stock of the situation, to ensure at least that if and
when the war ends he will be able to continue composing,
to consider whether the new regime which will inevitably
follow the war will be good for his art or bad and to bestir
himself, even at the risk of losing a few hours from his
manuscripts to help forward a desirable end?

How much does the artist owe to himself and how much
to the community? Or, to put it in another way, how far is
it true that the artist in serving himself ultimately serves
the community? This is possibly the case in normal times;
unless the artist is true to himself he cannot but be false

to any man. But times at present are not normal. I suppose that even the most self-absorbed composer would hardly go on writing music if his house was on fire; at all events he would gather up his manuscript sheets and take them to a place of safety. The artist must condition his inspiration by the nature of his material. What will be the musical material on which the composer of the future can count? It will be no use writing elaborate orchestral pieces if there are no orchestras left to play them, or subtle string quartets if there are no subtle instrumentalists available.

One thing, I think, we can be sure of, no bombs or blockades can rob us of our vocal chords; there will always remain for us the oldest and greatest of musical instruments, the human voice. Is it not possible that the quality of our inspiration and the nature of our material will meet here? Surely the most other-worldly composer must take thought for these things.

At the other end of the scale are those composers who feel that music in wartime is just an impossibility, either because the present unrest inhibits for them that serenity of mind which is essential for artistic invention, or because they are obsessed with the idea that they must do something 'useful' and that composing music is not 'useful'. It is to me, a doubtful point whether this salving of one's conscience by 'doing one's bit' is not a form of cowardice, but if the necessary calmness of mind can be obtained in no other way let the artist by all means drive an ambulance or sit in a telephone box for a sufficient number of hours to enable him to return with an untroubled mind to the things of the spirit.

I have up to now taken it for granted that music is not 'useful'. How far is this true? It is certainly, to my mind, one of the glories of the art of music that it can be put to no practical use. Poets can be used for propaganda, painters for camouflage, architects for machine-gun posts, but music is purely of the spirit and seems to have no place in the world of alarms and excursions. Would it not indeed be better for music to keep out of the struggle and reserve for us a place where sanity can again find a home when she returns to her own?

Nevertheless, the composer feels that he would like to be able to serve the community directly through his craft if not through his art. Before a man can become a good artist he must have become a good craftsman. Are there not ways in which the composer without derogating from his art, without being untrue to himself, but still without that entire disregard for his fellows which characterizes the artist in his supreme moments, use his skill, his knowledge, his sense of beauty in the service of his fellow men?

Composers are, perhaps, too apt to think only in terms of the very highly skilled executant, but cannot they in present circumstances think of the needs of the modest amateur, the parties of A.R.P. workers who have to spend long hours waiting for an ambulance call that never comes, the group of nurses eating their hearts out in an empty hospital, the business man and his family forced by the black-out and the petrol ration to spend their leisure hours at home. Would it not be a worthy object of the composer's skill to provide for these modest executants music worthy of their artistic imagination, but not beyond their technical skill? These very limitations may be the salvation of the composer.

It is right even to learn from the enemy. There has been in Germany of late years a 'Home Music' movement. Some of the best-known composers have occupied their time and their talents in arranging and composing music for the amateur to play in his own home. I should like to see this idea developed here—music for every fortuitous combination of instruments which may happen to be assembled in a parlour or a dug-out, with a part for anyone who happens to drop in. Why should we confine ourselves to the stereotyped string quartet or pianoforte trio? Why should the voice be always accompanied by the pianoforte? There seem to me great possibilities in voices and instruments in combination. Our old Madrigalists marked their works 'Apt for voices or viols', we could develop this; that rare bird the tenor could be replaced by a viola or clarinet, a weak soprano could be doubled by a flute and—(I hardly dare to breathe it)—the contralto part might be played on a saxophone. New material stimulates new ideas. Might not all these possibilities be a source of inspiration?

Art is a compromise between what we want to achieve and what circumstances allow us to achieve. It is out of these very compromises that the supreme art often springs; the highest comes when you least expect it. There is a delightful phantasy by Maurice Baring in which he imagines Shakespeare and his Company rehearsing *Macbeth*. The principal actor complains there is not enough 'fat' in his part, whereupon Shakespeare goes into a corner and hurriedly scribbles a dozen more lines for him beginning 'Tomorrow and tomorrow and tomorrow'. That is how great art often grows, by accident, while we think we are doing something else—often as a supply to meet a demand.

The great English Madrigal school grew up because singing round the supper table was fashionable and people demanded something to sing. Nowadays with our War limitations upon us, with concerts few and far between, with the B.B.C. ration of one symphony a week, home music will again come into its own. Is it altogether beneath the dignity of the young composer to meet that demand? These young composers are having a bad time now, no one seems to want them—there seems to be no midway between Beethoven and Sandy Macpherson. This may be true as far as public music is concerned, but how about the musician in the house? To write for the amateur may limit the scope, but it need not dim the inspiration of the composers. The amateur player, also, has his duty toward the young composer. Let him welcome and encourage him. In so doing, who knows that he may not entertain an angel unawares?

X

VAUGHAN WILLIAMS'S TALK ON PARRY AND STANFORD, 1957

WITH the permission of the organizers of this Concourse*
and by your leave, Mr. Chairman, I propose to enlarge the
scope of this talk so as to include Hubert Parry as well as
Charles Villiers Stanford. In my early days these two stood
together as the two forward-looking English musicians.
Nowadays the bright young things of music seem to have
forgotten them,—they do not even know how to spell
Stanford's name! But in my belief these two will come back
to us when many of our latest blunderbusses have proved
mere flashes in the pan.

I had the honour to be a pupil of both these great men.
I went to Parry as a lad of seventeen, and naturally absorbed
him wholesale. Then came three years at Cambridge and
technical instruction from Charles Wood and others, so that
by the time I became a pupil of Stanford's I was musically
more mature and did not fall under his spell as completely
as I did under that of Parry.

Let us take Parry first. Many more recent writers, for
instance Arnold Bax and Philip Heseltine, entirely misunderstood Parry; they were deceived by his rubicund bon-
homie and imagined that he had the mind, as he had the
appearance, of a country squire. The fact is that Parry had
a highly nervous temperament. He was in early days a
thinker with very advanced views. I remember, for example, how in the early nineties he accepted Ibsen with
delight. He was one of the early champions of Wagner when
other thinkers in this country were still calling him impious.

*During the winter of 1957 the Composers' Concourse organized a
series of lectures on Composers as Teachers.

His life of Wagner, published in the early eighties in his
Studies of Great Composers, is masterly, putting him in his
high place, long before the time when Bernard Shaw and
his satellites imagined that they had discovered him. His
early radicalism subsided in later years to a broad-minded
conservatism. He would take the trouble to listen to Schoenberg, even in his old age. Naturally he did not like him, but
he was willing to test him; though, after hearing the *Five
Orchestral Pieces* he is reported to have said 'I can stand
this fellow when he is loud, it is when he is soft he is so
obscene.'

In 1891 when I first went to Parry he was indeed an
out-and-out radical both in art and life. He introduced me
to Wagner and Brahms—which was quite contrary to
curricula then obtaining in academies. He showed me the
greatness of Bach and Beethoven as compared with Handel
and Mendelssohn. He once discovered with horror that I did
not know the finale of Beethoven's Appassionata Sonata, so
he sat down and played it to me, pointing out as he went on,
how the development grew to a great climax. It was a
wonderful performance and I shall never forget it.

In the year 1891 there were early performances of
Siegfried, under Mahler, and Parry generously lent me a
copy of the pianoforte score, [which was] hard to obtain in
those days. I remember how amused, but pleased, he was
when I showed him a song which I thought I had composed,
but was really a passage out of the third act of *Siegfried*. It
was a setting of Browning's *Summum bonum*. He praised its
insight, but said it was too much like *Siegfried* to be allowed
to pass!

Parry was always on the look-out for what was 'characteristic'—even if he disliked the music he would praise it if
he saw that it had character. I remember once I showed him
a piece in which, by pure carelessness, I had repeated a note
in a scale passage; Parry, as his custom was, had kept the
piece back to look at it in the week, and he said to me 'I have
been looking at that passage for a long time to see if it was

just accident, or something characteristic.' I nearly died of shame.

Parry never tried to divorce art from life: he once said to me 'Write choral music as befits an Englishman and a democrat.' This attitude towards art led to an almost moral hatred of mere luscious sound. It has been said that Parry's orchestration was bad; there may have been occasional carelessness and hurry, but I think the truth was that he occasionally went too far in mere eschewal of orchestral effects. Some years ago I was sitting next to Elgar at a rehearsal of Parry's *Symphonic Variations*, I said 'I suppose many people would call this bad orchestration.' Elgar replied angrily 'Of course it's not bad orchestration; the music could have been scored in no other way.'

Parry's generosity is well known: I have already told you how he used to lend valuable music to his pupils, which was not always returned. The story of Parry and the Elgar *Variations* is well known, though it was persistently ignored by Bernard Shaw in his attempts to draw a picture of Elgar persecuted by mysterious people whom he invented and called 'The Academic Clique'. But perhaps the following story is not so well known; Parry had for a pupil Richard Walthew, who one day showed him a setting of Browning's *Pied Piper*. Parry thought so well of it that he determined to try to get it a public performance. But Parry had already nearly finished a setting of his own of the same words. What did Parry do? He just put his own setting away in a drawer and said nothing about it to Walthew for whom he obtained his public performance. I think it was twenty years before Parry allowed his own setting to be performed.

Parry was a thinker on music, which he connected, not only with life, but with other aspects of philosophy and science. When Parry was a young man the Darwinian controversy was in full swing. He became a follower of Herbert Spencer and decided to find out how far music, as well as the rest of life, followed the laws of evolution. These thoughts he embodied in his great book, *The Evolution of the Art of Music*, in which he proves, conclusively to most people, that Beethoven's Ninth Symphony, for example, is not an isolated phenomenon, but a highly developed stage of a process of evolution which can be traced back to the primitive folk-songs of our people. I understand that there has grown up among our younger musicians a sort of musical fundamentalism, with its garden of Eden all complete; according to this theory we are to believe, I suppose, that a Beethoven symphony is not a development but a degenerate relic of angelic strains of some musical Adam and Eve. I suppose that these young people will say with Disraeli that they are on the side of the angels.

What about Parry as a composer? Potentially, I believe, he was among the greatest. But something stood in the way of complete realization. There is however one outstanding exception. I fully believe—and keeping the achievements of Byrd, Purcell, and Elgar firmly before my eyes,—*Blest Pair of Sirens* is the finest musical work that has come out of these islands.

Stanford in many ways was the opposite of Parry. Parry is sometimes musically inarticulate and clumsy. Stanford was occasionally too clever. His very facility sometimes betrayed him. He could, at will, adopt the technique of any composer he chose—as in *The Middle Watch*, where he beats Delius at his own game. But in such works as the *Stabat Mater* and the *Requiem* and some of his songs we find Stanford thinking his own beautiful thoughts in his own beautiful way. His very facility prevented him from knowing when he was genuinely inspired and when his work was routine stuff. Therefore we have to confess that some of his enormous output is dull and uninspired. But is this not true also of Beethoven and Bach? The great composer goes in for mass-production. He does not wait for the spark from Heaven to fall, otherwise he might, like the scholar gypsy, wander round the country for ever, always searching but never finding. I believe that every composer can achieve something, even a small song, which no one else could do as well; but it must come out of a mass of often uninspired stuff; the composer must not stand waiting for a miracle to happen.

In 1952 we had occasion to celebrate the centenary of Stanford's birth. In any continental country a composer of Stanford's calibre would have been celebrated with performances in every opera house in the country. We have only two opera houses here, but even they could not give us an opportunity of hearing such splendid works, full of possibilities of popularity, as *Much Ado* and *Shamus O'Brien*. Instead they chose rather to shake the dead bones of *Norma* and Saint-Saëns's *Samson et Dalila*.

Stanford achieved a certain distinction as a conductor. He had of course no truck with the ideas of the temperamental director. His object was to present faithfully what the composer intended. For that reason he was labelled as 'academic' by certain silly journalists who complained that he 'lacked imaginative fancy'—which meant apparently that he gave his audiences what he believed the composer meant, and not what he thought he ought to have meant. Against this let me set the opinion of Eugene Goossens, himself a distinguished conductor, who as a student at the Royal College of Music had played the violin in the orchestra under Stanford's beat. Goossens told me that in his opinion Stanford was the finest interpreter of Brahms that he had ever heard.

I have just mentioned the word 'academic'. It was the fashion among a certain class of journalist about fifty years ago to describe Parry, Stanford and others who ruled at the Royal College of Music as 'academic', which apparently meant that they founded the emotion of their music on knowledge, and not on mere sensation. To these critics, admiration of Brahms was equivalent to dry-as-dust pedantry. If they are alive today they must feel rather foolish when they see Brahms filling the house at a Promenade concert.

Stanford is best known to the general public by his arrangements of Irish melodies. He had made an exhaustive study of Petrie, Bunting, and other Irish collections, for he realized, as we all should, that vital art must spring from its own soil. I am far from saying that we have all got to write sham folk-songs; neither Parry nor Elgar, so far as I know ever used an actual English folk-song in their work. But we do feel that the same circumstances which produced our beautiful English folk-songs also produced their music, founded as it should be on our own history, our own customs, our own incomparable landscape, even perhaps our undependable weather and our abominable food. The youngest generation of composers profess not to believe in folk-song, but for the last fifty years we have been constantly in touch with it and they can no more help being influenced by it than by their own language.

If I might give a word of advice to young composers I would say 'learn the elements of your art at home; then, only then, when you feel sure of what you want to do, and feel the ability to do it, go and rub noses with the composers of other lands and see what you can learn from them. You may say that you do not want to be national, but that you want to be international. You will not achieve this by denying your own country from the start. If you subscribe to that extremely foolish description of music as a universal language, you will find that you have achieved nothing better than a standardized and emasculated cosmopolitanism which will mean nothing to you nor to those whose mannerisms you have been aping.'

The great universal figures of every art, such as Shakespeare, Bach, and Velasquez have also been the most intensely national. Shakespeare's clowns, even when they have Italian names and are nominally living in Italy, are purely English countrymen. Who could be more English than Dickens? And yet he has achieved popularity even in Russia. It was from the painting of that very English artist, Constable, that the whole French Impressionist movement grew. In this connection may I quote you a passage from an author who, so far as I know, knew little about music, and

H.R.–H

certainly knew nothing about folk song. Virginia Woolf
writes as follows:

> Masterpieces are not single and solitary births, they are the
> outcome of many years thinking in common, of thinking by the
> body of the people so that the experience of the many is behind
> the single voice.

Now let us turn to Stanford as a teacher. We cannot
consider him as a teacher without thinking of him as a man.
He was a true Irishman, quarrelsome and at the same time
lovable and generous. Though artistically we were poles
apart, I had for him that affection which certain types of
man seem to call up. He was intolerant and narrow-minded,
and it was this, I think, which made him a good teacher. If
a thing was wrong, it was wrong; if it was right it was right,
and there was no question about it. It is fatal for a teacher
to say, even mentally, to a pupil 'well perhaps you are right
after all.' Stanford was often cruel in his judgements and
the more sensitive among his pupils wilted under his
methods and found comfort under a more soft-hearted
teacher. I remember I once showed Stanford the slow
movement of a string quartet. I had worked feverishly at it,
and, like every other young composer, thought not only
that it was the finest piece that had ever been written, and
that my teacher would fall on his knees and embrace me,
but that it was also my swan song. Now what would Parry
have done in a case like this? He would have pored over it
for a long time in hopes of finding something characteristic
and, even if he disliked the piece as a whole, would try to
find some point to praise. Stanford dismissed it with a curt
'All rot, me boy!' This was cruel but salutary. So far as I can
remember, he was quite right. Luckily the piece was lost
years ago.

Stanford's teaching was constructive. He was not content
to criticize what his pupils brought him, but he set them
tasks to perform in order to strengthen certain parts of their
work. When I was with him at the Royal College he had

just been back to school with Rockstro, studying all over again what was then known as modal counterpoint. This study had fascinated him, and partly for this reason and partly to counteract a growing tendency to Tchaikovskian lusciousness which he discovered among his pupils, he set them to work writing masses and motets in strict modal counterpoint. I was let off this discipline because Stanford found that I was too far gone in the modes already. Also, he found in my work too much seriousness and even stodginess; so he decided that I must write a waltz. True to my creed I showed him a modal waltz!

Stanford's own music is the music of an educated man. He had formed his style partly on the songs of his native land and partly on the songs of the great masters. His musical style might be compared with the literary style of Matthew Arnold, and it was this sense of style that he passed on, often unconsciously, to his pupils. When I was Stanford's pupil I made the great mistake of fighting my teacher. A great deal of our meagre lesson time was occupied with the discussion of whether one of my progressions was damnably ugly or not, which time might have more profitably been spent on the larger issues. Anything crude or clumsy,—or 'ugly,' as he called it—was anathema to Stanford. He accused me once of all the crudities in Blow mentioned in Burney's History.

I had not read Burney, but probably if I had read it I should have found I had done just what Stanford accused me of. The way to get the best out of instruction is to surrender oneself, mind and soul, to one's instructor and to try to learn his methods without intruding one's own personality. Young students are much too fond of their own personalities. In the merest harmony exercises they insist on keeping all their clumsy progressions because that is what they 'felt', forgetting that art cannot mature unless the craft matures along side of it. Stanford would sometimes sigh deeply when I brought him my week's work and say he was hoping against hope! Nevertheless, his deeds were better than his words, and it was he who persuaded the Leeds Festival to perform my *Sea Symphony*.

The value of lessons with a great teacher cannot be computed in terms of what he said, or what you did, but in terms of some intangible contact with his mind and character. With Stanford I felt I was in the presence of a lovable, powerful and enthralling mind; this helped me more than any amount of technical instruction.

POSTSCRIPT

EHEU FUGACES . . .

Horace, Odes II, xiv. 1.

Swiftly they pass, the flying years,
no prayers can stay their course,
here is the road each man must tread
be he of royal blood or lowly birth.
Vainly we shun the battles' roar
the perilous sea, the fever-laden breezes,
soon shall we reach our journey's end
and trembling cross the narrow stream of death.
Land, house and wife must all be left,
the cherished trees be all cut down,
strangers shall lord it in our home
and squander all our store.

Translated by Vaughan Williams
for the Abinger Pageant, 1938.

RALPH VAUGHAN WILLIAMS

List of works mentioned in the text

Title	*Publisher*
Bucolic Suite.	MS discarded
Concerto Accademico, for violin and string orchestra.	Oxford University Press
Concerto for pianoforte and orchestra.	Oxford University Press
Flos Campi, suite for solo viola, small chorus, and small orchestra.	Oxford University Press
Four Hymns, for tenor, viola, and string orchestra.	Boosey and Hawkes
Garden of Proserpine, The.	MS. discarded
Heroic Elegy.	MS. discarded
Job. A masque for dancing.	Oxford University Press
London Symphony, A.	Stainer and Bell
Magnificat, for contralto solo, women's chorus and orchestra.	Oxford University Press
Mass.	MS. destroyed
Mass in G minor, for soli and double chorus.	Curwen
Pastoral Symphony.	Curwen
Sancta Civitas. Oratorio for tenor, baritone, chorus, semi-chorus, and orchestra.	Curwen
Sea Symphony, A. For soprano and baritone, chorus, and orchestra.	Stainer and Bell
Sentimental Romance.	MS. destroyed
Symphonic Rhapsody.	MS. destroyed
Symphony No 4 in F minor.	Oxford University Press

GUSTAV HOLST

List of works mentioned in the text

Opus	Date	Title	Publisher
9b	1900	Ave Maria, for unaccompanied female voices in eight parts.	Bosworth
51	1930	Choral Fantasia, for soprano solo, chorus, organ, strings, brass, and percussion.	Curwen
41	1923–4	Choral Symphony, for soprano solo, chorus, and orchestra.	Novello
30	1910–12	Cloud Messenger, The. Ode for chorus and orchestra.	Novello
—	1932	David's Lament for Jonathan. Canon for equal voices, unaccompanied.	Curwen
49	1929	Double Concerto, for two violins and orchestra.	Curwen
47	1927	Egdon Heath, for orchestra.	Novello
—	1932	Fields of Sorrow, The. Canon for equal voices, unaccompanied.	Curwen
52	1930	Hammersmith. Prelude and Scherzo for orchestra.	Boosey and Hawkes
37	1917	Hymn of Jesus, The. For two choruses, semi-chorus, and orchestra.	Stainer and Bell
—	1931	Intercession. Chorus for male voices with string accompaniment.	Boosey and Hawkes
15	1902	Invocation to Dawn, for baritone and piano.	MS.*
—	1932	Lovely Venus. Canon for equal voices, unaccompanied.	Curwen
38	1919	Ode to Death, for chorus and orchestra.	Novello
6	1898	Ornulf's Drapa. Scena for baritone and orchestra.	MS.*
23	1899– 1906	Sita. Opera in three acts.	MS.*
—	1925	Terzetto, for flute, oboe, and viola.	Chester
22	1906	Two Songs without Words, for small orchestra.	Novello
50	1929–30	Wandering Scholar, The. Opera in one act.	MS.
—	1930–1	Welsh Folk Songs arranged for unaccompanied chorus.	Curwen
11	1901–2	Youth's Choice, The. Opera.	MS.*

*These manuscripts are now in the British Museum.

INDEX

INDEX

(References to notes include editorial notes in the text as well as footnotes.)

St Paul's Girls' School, xiii, 44n,
  45, 49n, 64, 74
Sancta Civitas, 63
Schoenberg, 80, 95
Schubert, 17, 27, 32, 52, 56
Schumann, 20, 29–33
Scottish Orchestra, xiii, 2n, 13, 17,
  36
Sea Symphony, A, 40, 102
Shakespeare, 93, 99
Sharp, Cecil, 38
Sharp, Evelyn, 35n
Shaw, George Bernard, 67, 95, 96
Silk, Dorothy, 61, 65, 85
Sir John In Love, 35n
Sita, 8, 12, 17, 40, 41
Spencer, Herbert, 96
Stanford, Sir Charles Villiers, x,
  xi, 1, 21, 24, 41, 94–102
Strauss, Johann, 55
Strauss, Richard, 20, 25
Suddaby, Elsie, 79
Symphonic Rhapsody, 9n
Symphony No. 4, 80, 81, 84
Synge, J. M., 35n
Tallis, 39
Tchaikovsky, 13
Terzetto, 83
Thaxted, 44n, 45, 46
Thompson, Francis, 6
Three Choirs Festival, 77n

Titian, 25
Trinity College, Cambridge, xii
Two Songs without Words, 40
University Extension Lectures, xii
Van der Weyden, 23
Van Dieren, Bernard, 62
Van Eyck, 23
Vaughan Williams, Adeline (*née*
  Fisher), xii, 3n, 25n, 44, 81
Velasquez, 99
Veronese, 23, 25
Vocalist, The, xi, xii
Wagner, x, 1, 3n, 7, 12, 18, 20,
  23, 24, 25, 28, 33, 94, 95
Walküre, Die, 1
Walthew, Richard, 96
Wandering Scholar, The, 75
Weber, 32
Webern, 80
Weelkes, 52–55
Welsh Folk Songs, 77
Wesley, Samuel, 55–56
White Viennese Band, 2n, 12n
Wilson, Sir Steuart, 79
Wood, Charles, 94
Wood, Sir Henry J., 2, 12, 21, 36
Woolf, Virginia, 100
Wurm, Stanislas, 12, 16, 17, 21,
  24
Yale University, 66, 72
Youth's Choice, The, 6